RETURN
Poems Collected and New

Bilingual Press/Editorial Bilingüe

General Editor
Gary D. Keller

Managing Editor
Karen S. Van Hooft

Senior Editor
Mary M. Keller

Editorial Board
Juan Goytisolo
Francisco Jiménez
Eduardo Rivera
Severo Sarduy
Mario Vargas Llosa

Address
Bilingual Press
Department of Foreign Languages
and Bilingual Studies
106 Ford Hall
EASTERN MICHIGAN UNIVERSITY
Ypsilanti, Michigan 48197
313-487-0042

ALURISTA

RETURN
Poems Collected and New

Bilingual Press/Editorial Bilingüe
YPSILANTI, MICHIGAN

ISBN: 0-916950-24-7

Library of Congress Catalog Card Number: 81-68424

PRINTED IN THE UNITED STATES OF AMERICA

Cover design by Christopher J. Bidlack

Drawing of author (back cover) by Sergio C. Gaytán, 1980.

TABLE OF CONTENTS

SERPIENTE

CONEJO

vi

VENADO

dawn's eye *(1979-1981)*

ALURISTA, POETA-ANTROPOLOGO, AND THE RECUPERATION OF THE CHICANO IDENTITY

Gary D. Keller

This volume brings together one of Alurista's earliest and most celebrated works, *Nationchild plumaroja* (1972), and his latest book of poems, *Dawn's Eye*. Some of those who have studied Alurista's literary production over the last ten years or so—¡han pasado los años!—have noted the development and change of that obra over the decade. They have highlighted the defiant social protest in *Floricanto en Aztlán* (1971); the alienation with USA and the harking back to Amerindia through cultural and thematic motifs as well as generic forms (chants and songs) in *Nationchild*; the expression, mostly in Spanish, of the spiritual rebirth of the Hispanic and Chicano world as well as the natural world in *Timespace huracán* (1976); the use of Hispanicized spelling of English (jai-fai, controlar morras [control more ass], etc.) and the inclusion of cuentos in *A'nque;* and the extreme linguistic experimentation with Spanish and English glyphs and sounds in *Spik in Glyph?* (1981). However, at the same time, there has often been a pointing to the constants in Alurista's obra. This would be a good occasion, the published juxtaposition of both his second and his latest book, to shed light on some of those qualities, both thematic and stylistic, which in my judgment contribute to the clearly recognizable poetic persona of Alurista.

Many writers have explored the Chicano identity—thematically this is the most prominent feature of our creative production. The key notion in Alurista's identity exploration for me is one that I have highlighted in the title of this essay and in its development and exposition: recuperation—a process of delving into, elucidating, and disabusing facets of self which were there all along, but which like certain Palenques and Uxmales required the efforts of the visionary archaeologist to unearth. Alurista has a great capacity for teasing out the component strands of lo nuestro. Indeed, he is one of the great teasers of Chicano poetry!

Within this circumscribed context of discussing Alurista's anthropological poetic, I also take the opportunity to give a brief philological orientation to both Alurista and the texts published here. It should be stated from the onset, however, that the major information resource in this book about Alurista's work is the comprehensive bibliography Tina Eger has prepared. Finally, I should state that I write this essay from the perspective of an estudioso who is also, a veces, poeta, and I will take occasionally the licenses and liberties—not with facts, but with language—that can be proffered only to the latter.

Alurista, antropólogo

Alurista (nom de plume of Alberto Baltazar Urista) was born in Mexico City in 1947 and moved to San Diego—donde se ha quedado, más o menos—at the age of thirteen. I mention these facts because I think it important to highlight, in relationship to his work, his natal origins as well as the continued physical proximity of the republic of Mexico in his life. In paraphrase of what Unamuno once said about Spain, that Africa begins with the Pyrenees, I say of my beloved and behated San Diego, or better yet, of Nuestra Señora de Los Angeles, that it is the beginning of Mexico, Amerindia, the psychological birthplace of a Chicano Aztlán. Other Chicano poets such as Sergio Elizondo and Abelardo Delgado were born in Mexico, but for Alurista I think this datum has more genuine relevance. Apart from being un hombre muy leído y escribido como decíamos en Tijuana/San Dedo, and all critics will have to take seriously into account that depth of reading and research that our poet has undertaken as well as its variety and eclecticism—Marcuse and Buddhism, mathematics and the mathematics of Hunab Ku, and so on—it appears that Alurista has read and appreciated contemporary Mexican writers such as Octavio Paz and Carlos Fuentes and certainly has digested significant amounts of Aztec-Toltec and Mayan creative literature, myth, philosophy, cosmogeny and history. Preferring not to mix nectar with water, I have refrained from quizzing Alurista or showing him an advance draft of this essay, but I do wonder how well he is acquainted, if at all, with secondary sources on Amerindia such as Fernando Benítez, *Los indios de México*; Ignacio Bernal, *Mexico Before Cortez*; Fray Diego Durán, *Historia de las Indias de Nueva España*; Angel María K. Garibay, *Epica náhuatl, Historia de la literatura náhuatl, Veinte himnos sacros de los nahuas*, and *Poesía náhuatl*; Edward Kissam and Michael Schmidt, *Flower and Song: Poems of the Aztec Peoples*; Miguel León-Portilla, *La filosofía náhuatl, estudiada en sus fuentes* and *Los antiguos mexicanos através de sus crónicas y cantares*; Helen O'Gorman, *Plantas y flores de méxico*; and Demetrio Sodi Pallares, *La literatura de los maya.*

The relationship between Alurista's work and that of Octavio Paz is also a worthy one to investigate. Guillermo Rojas (in an unpublished manuscript) has shown interesting comparisons between "Construyendo una balsa" (in *Nationchild*) and Octavio Paz's poem "Balcón" and feels that both *Floricanto* and *Nationchild*, which each consist of one hundred poems, seem to be modeled on Octavio Paz's *Centena*, a collection of one hundred poems. Rojas also has identified in Carlos Fuentes' essay "De Quetzalcóatl a Pepsicóatl" (*Tiempo Mexicano*) the inspiration for the characters Pepsicóatl and Cocacóatl which appear in Alurista's play *Dawn*.

The presence of Mexico, digo México, is overt in Alurista's poetry and it encompasses a wide range of historical periods, themes, folkways, and cultural motifs, as well as lexicon. For example, in "We've Played Cowboys" (*Floricanto*) it is the charro who is evoked:

> We've played cowboys
>   not knowing
> nuestros charros
>   and their countenance
> con trajes de gala
>   silver embroidery
> on black wool

In one of the poems in *Dawn's Eye* it is Calexico compared to Amsterdam,

>   calexico quivers, rattles
>   past sunsetting winds

> amsterdam longs for the warmth
> of a southern california crepúsculo

and constantly in Alurista's poetry there is the recognition of Mexican food and its implements—the evocation of salsa and comales, café and tazas de barro, coco, tortillas, chile verde and chile colorado, maíz, calabazas, and of course, ¿quién los iba a olvidar? chilaquiles,

> i had chilaquiles
>> to share in ollas de color — pintadas jarras
>> white man dug our spice and shun our breath
>> he came to us to eat
>> and ran

> (*Nationchild plumaroja*)

Yet, above all, it is the pre-Columbian element that characterizes our poet's mexicanidad and it is that component especially which I wish to survey since it is critical to understanding Alurista as a poeta-antropólogo. Alurista's is not an obra which seasons lightly with an occasional Quetzalcóatl or Tláloc! Here we are confronted with Tezcatlipoca, Mixcóatl, Ometeotl, Tonantzín, Tizoc, Xochitl, Ixtoc, Cuauhtémoc and Kukulkán.

Of course, words are only a part of this pre-Columbian connection. *Nationchild*, as anyone can attest who has glimpsed the first edition with its Amerindian pagination and art, bears witness to this. (Alurista requested Arabic rather than Mesoamerican numbering for the current edition.) Mesoamérica recuperated by a Chicano Aztlán is what our poet seeks. In an interview with Bruce-Novoa, Alurista responds to the question of whether or not he perceives his poetry as political:

> Of course my work is political. To be political is to be concerned with the welfare of the many. I am. But I don't think my work can be defined only as political, because it's political, it's scientific, it's psychological, it's spiritual, it's cultural. It's a lot of things, all at once. Some people say my poetry is protest poetry. No. It's also about reconstructing. To reconstruct ourselves, because being colonized people, the self that we possess, the view that we have, is colored by the colonization that we suffered, by the schooling that we have been subjected to.[1]

Reconstructing, reconstituting is what deeply interests Alurista and the Aztec/Toltec/Maya element is the prime body of lore that requires this act of recuperative poetic science. We have here a poet who is in a profound sense an anthropologist for his pueblo, for he has attempted and succeeded in restoring the sense of a pre-Columbian heritage to the Chicano. It is the observation of Luis Leal that Alurista was perhaps the first who at the level of literature and formal ideology (in contrast to popular usages, where earlier examples can be attested to) established—in 1968-69—the concept of a Chicano Aztlán: a symbol—cultural, political, geographic, and above all, mythic—of the aspirations of la Raza. Indeed, in 1969 the term is first mentioned in a Chicano document, one which Alurista had a major responsibility in formulating, *El Plan Espiritual de Aztlán*. The *Plan*, as Luis Leal recognizes, is significant,

> . . . because in it the Chicano recognizes his Aztec origins ("We, the Chicano inhabitants and civilizers of the northern land of Aztlán, from whence came our forefathers . . ."); because it establishes that Aztlán is the Mexican territory ceded to the United States in 1848, and because, following one of the basic ideas of the Mexican Revolution, it recognizes that the land belongs to those who work it ("Aztlán belongs to those that plant the seeds, water the fields, and gather the crops"); and finally, it identifies the Chicano with Aztlán ("We are a nation, we are a union of free pueblos, we are AZTLAN").[2]

In the following year, 1970, the first number of the journal *Aztlán* appeared. In it the *Plan* was published in both English and Spanish, the prologue to which was Alurista's "Poem in Lieu of a Preface."

<pre>
            it is said
                    that MOTECUHZOMA ILHUICAMINA
SENT
                    AN expedition
    looking for the NortherN
                mYthical land
    wherefrom the AZTECS CAME
                la TIERRA
                        dE
                    AztláN
                mYthical land for those
                who dream of roses and
    swallow thorns
</pre>

                    or for those who swallow thorns
            in powdered milk
      feeling guilty about smelling flowers
                              about looking for AztláN

The source of inspiration for this poem is Fray Diego Durán, *Historia de las Indias de Nueva España*, which perhaps our poet consulted directly but about which he could have learned from numerous post-colonial sources as well. In the following year (1971) Alurista edited *El ombligo de Aztlán: Anthology of Chicano Poetry* and published his own *Floricanto en Aztlán*.

It is not only the mythos of Aztlán that Alurista wants to resurrect. In the Bruce-Novoa interview our poet remarked about language that "Many of us are beginning to restore, or bring to life, some of the indigenous languages, such as Mayan and Náhuatl."[3] And subsequently in the interview:

> I don't think Chicano literature can be properly classified as Spanish or English literature, or North American literature. We use both languages. It's a little bit of both and it's neither. It's something in itself. It has its own existence and gives its own flower. It has its own root and its root, without doubt, from my point of view, is indigenous. Poetry is the traditional means of philosophical, theological, and scientific expression in the Indian world. The Indians wrote in poetry, not because they did not write prose, but simply because they thought that poetry was more realistic, more dialectic, more dynamic.[4]

Concerning literature, Alurista claims, "our literature promises more than any of the literatures of Central or South America. We are the belt between Anglo American and Indohispanic America."[5] In referring to our Weltanschauung, as it were, once again Alurista is drawn to an Amerindian, pre-Columbian reality: "Even if something appears to be static, like this table, science tells us, as the Mayans told us, no, this table is in full motion. Electrons moving around nuclei. Everything is in motion. Everything is alive and is part of the whole. We are one with the world."[6] And again:

> The name of God among the Mayans was Hunab Ku. Hunab Ku was not a metaphysical god, or a metaphysical idea which had to be accepted solely through faith, but rather the only giver of measure and movement. Hunab Ku was a mathematical equation. Or, rather, religion was science and science religion. In this man-

ner I consider my poetry to be mathematics, and mathematics to be poetry.[7]

There is a complication and a caution that must be made, however, when comparing Alurista to the anthropologist in his delving into and exposing Amerindia so that it may be incorporated into a Chicano Aztlán. Alurista's stance toward the pre-Columbian peoples, while based on considerable reading and knowledge, is fundamentally romantic. Ybarra-Frausto has judged the recuperation of the pre-Columbian past by Chicano writers to be a mixed blessing:

> Alurista's recovery of these sources was not an isolated phenomenon but part of a pervasive validation of pre-Columbian heritage as an integral part of the Chicano Movement. At its best, this linkage with a non-European cultural tradition provided abundant mythic and symbolic structures for artists, writers, and intellectuals. At its worst, it inspired a romantic "neo-indigenism" designed to make barrio vatos think of themselves as descendants of Aztec nobility without focusing on the basic realities of pre-Hispanic life. Furthermore, the glorification of a remote past tended to obscure the historical contradictions of Indio-Chicano relationships within the United States.[8]

Similar sentiments are expressed by Juan Rodríguez in his study, "La búsqueda de identidad y sus motivos en la literatura chicana."

> Este nuevo afán nos lleva a otra manifestación de la búsqueda: el volver al pasado en busca del *ubi sunt*, del *là-bas*, del paraíso perdido en el que el chicano, se supone, gozaba de su ser completo, poseía una identidad. En algunas obras este afán se resuelve en empeño completamente utópico. La máxima y más desarrollada realización de esto se da en el mito de Aztlán, que si bien fue ingeniosa y oportunamente rescatado del olvido por el vate Alurista (*Floricanto en Aztlán*), en nuestros días ya se ha convertido en bagaje demasiado pesado, para el movimiento chicano.[9]

The same criticism has been leveled against the Teatro Campesino upon the establishment of its *mitos*, which were intended, according to Luis Valdez, to function as cuates or dramatic twins to the *actos*. A rather extensive polemic has brewed about the *mitos*.[10] For example, one of the more trenchant critics, Brazilian dramatist Augusto Boal, warns against the danger of idealizing and romanticizing the past, turning the search for roots into an "ahistorical fiction," turning from the fact that pre-Hispanic Amerindian society had numerous defects such as the practice of human sacrifice (often for political rather than religious ends—the latter being repulsive enough in their own right), government by hereditary practice, extreme hierarchical class structure, and the suppression of women. Boal particularly objects to the editorial statement of the *Teatro Campesino* magazine that speaks of "the Indian pre-Hispanic spirit, a spirit free from egoism, full of equality and struggle. It is a culture of love, of brotherhood, of support." To return to Juan Rodríguez's essay (which is also critical of the *mitos* on the same grounds as Boal), the final criticism cuts a broad swath across writers:

> . . . el viaje al pasado resulta . . . inútil. Por un lado termina en mitos indígenas tan remotos que pierden su sentido benéfico original; sólo otorgan una identidad hollywoodesca o libresca, en todo caso ajena a la realidad concreta del chicano (*Floricanto en Aztlán*). Por otro lado da a un mundo místico, cerrado, fabricado en torno a la superstición (*Bless Me, Ultima*). En otros casos, y son los más, no se encuentra, por supuesto, ningún paraíso perdido . . . sino que se da con la misma enajenación de siempre (*Peregrinos de Aztlán*).
> Consecuentemente el viaje termina como tiene que terminar: en la frustración; pues únicamente así puede terminar un viaje a ciegas en el cual es imposible reconocer el fin, en el cual jamás se está consciente de haber llegado porque en realidad no hay a-dónde llegar, es decir, no hay paraíso perdido.[11]

Alurista is not completely invulnerable to the criticism of a romantic neo-indigenism as well as a utopian return to an ahistorical mythos, but the issue is a complex one, which when analyzed, I believe, ultimately favors the cause of our poeta-antropólogo. We must note that at no time did Alurista use the mother lode of Amerindian lore in an uncritical way vis-à-vis the present. It is imperative to highlight the fact that for Alurista, indigenista literary content functioned on behalf of his "cultural guerrilla" movement, his cadre of Toltecas en Aztlán which he envisioned as being trained to use art as a weapon in the struggle for social justice and cultural revolution. As I will show in more detail in the following section on Alurista's poetics, pre-Columbian religion, philosophy and cosmogeny, music, dancing, flower worship, communal ceremony and ritual were all applied in his poems to the goal of evoking a sense of ethnic and class consciousness among the Chicano people. As I have partially cited earlier, Alurista responded to Bruce-Novoa's question about the political nature of his work and life in a manner which encompassed pre-Hispanic Amerindia into a spiritual and political program of reconstitution in the hoy día:

> We have to give ourselves the responsibility of constructing a vision of the world that is truly ours, not a colonized vision of the world. An independent, liberated view of reality. If we paint a more humanistic world to live in, we will construct that world. If we paint a nightmare, we'll live in a nightmare. Therefore my poetry is not only political, it's psychological, it's spiritual. It is multidimensional. I don't think it can be called just protest poetry. I'm also trying to nurture, to cultivate my heart as well as the heart of my people, so that we can reconstruct our selves.[12]

Alurista's poetry—including his use of Amerindia—has been critical, basically constructive and progressive, left-leaning in its call for decolonization, and iconoclastic in its superimposition of Toltec/Aztec and Mayan deities and concepts over those elements of Christianity which he felt were oppressive of el pueblo.

Moreover, Alurista's work can be seen as a reaction against vague, surface, inchoate pan-indigenismo, which has always existed in Mexico and in Aztlán as well. Octavio Romano both describes and well represents this phenomenon in his essay, "The Historical and Intellectual Presence of the Mexican Americans."

> . . . symbolically, the Indian penetrates throughout, and permeates, major aspects of Mexican-American life, and hardly a barrio exists that does not have someone who is nicknamed "El Indio" or "Los Indios." . . . On occasion los matachines still make their Indian appearance in churches and Aztec legends still pictorially tell and retell their stories in barrio living rooms, in kitchens, in bars, restaurants, tortillerías and Chicano newspapers. The stern face of Don Benito Juárez still peers out of books, still surveys living rooms and still takes a place of prominence in many Sociedad Mutualista halls and in the minds of men throughout the Southwest. Small wonder then, that several hundred years after the totally indigenous existence of Mexico, the reference is still made to these roots and origins in the Mexican-American community. . . . The Indian is root and origin, past and present,

virtually timeless in his barrio manifestations—a timeless symbol of opposition to cultural imperialism.[13]

Alurista, like a true archaeologist, surpassed streetwise, surface, and shallow barrio glimmerings of lo indio. He investigated in depth and with substance the mythic, philosophic, religious, and social roots of Amerindia, exposed them to a wide sector of Chicano society, and framed them for incorporation into el movimiento itself. His was an aspiration for social justice and cultural renewal founded on a more sharply defined Chicano identity that required a deeper understanding of Amerindia, of Aztlán.

Another point needs to be made about the myth of Aztlán and its relationship to alleged futile voyages for lost paradises. The Aztlán myth that Alurista was so instrumental in fostering is not really subject to the criticism of nostalgia or evasiveness, at least on historical grounds, because to do justice to its original integrity it must always entertain the notion of a paraíso perdido. The notion of Aztlán as a lost paradise is consistent with Náhuatl mythology as recorded by Fray Diego Durán and by other chroniclers as well. Moreover, Alurista is the one who does not "return" to a solipsistic lost paradise but brings it to el pueblo, captures its quintessence and harnesses it in service of el movimiento. From the point of view of the social architect, revolutionary, or ideologue, the pervasive acceptance that the notion of Aztlán and its allied term "Raza" have had across all sectors of Chicano society show that Alurista's goals and whatever contribution he made to furthering them have been realized in a momentously effective fashion, rendering our poet once again invulnerable to the charge of futile nostalgias.

In sum, Alurista accomplished the positive goal of doing justice to the original Náhuatl sense of Aztlán while at the same time extrapolating Amerindian lore into the present in a fashion that was socially progressive and consciousness-raising. In addition, by means of his poetry he greatly broadened the understanding of Amerindia, perhaps not among all of el pueblo (we all know Aztlán but we don't all recite poetry), but certainly among a wide segment of educated Chicano society.

Alurista is vulnerable to the charge of romantic neo-indigenism only because while he went much further than most, he did not go far enough in his anthropological pursuits. Also, probably, he was protective of Amerindia in the ways that many Mexicans (once again the natal origins) have been. He is vulnerable to not representing the past as critically as he has engaged the present.

To be more specific about this, while nineteenth-century Latin American writers such as Juan León Mera (*Cumandá*) and José María Heredia (*Moctezuma, Xicoténcatl*), taking their cues from continental romantics like Chateaubriand, turned el indio into a romantic "noble savage," Alurista has made of him (and definitely not her!) a twentieth-century romantic "noble savant." What Alurista mostly neglects when contrasting pre-Hispanic Amerindia with the heartless gabacho nowadays are the contradictions inherent in his juxtaposition, caused by the fact of severe social and class inequities, human sacrifices, and the suppression of women typical of indigenista society. Alurista does not proceed in so blithe and perhaps ingenuously romantic a fashion as Luis Omar Salinas, who proclaims an "Aztec Angel." On the contrary, following the usual Mexican anthro-politic toward its pre-Columbian pueblos he more often exalts Toltecas over Aztecas, the latter being not only barbarian *arrivistes* who didn't even reach Tula from the North until the 12th century A.D., but also notable for their cruelties and outrages during certain periods of their history. (With the possible exception of *Yo soy Joaquín*, Chicano thought and literary inspiration, in contrast to mother Mexico's, hasn't quite fully digested the reasons for an indio alliance with Cortés. Its upshots in Mexican thought lead to certain strands such as Vasconcelos' exaltation of la Raza Cósmica as well as a defense of malinchismo by certain Mexican feminists. I predict the Chicano pen, particularly of feminists, will soon cultivate such themes.)

A more objective and comprehensive anthropologist, one perhaps less concerned with protecting the embryonic Chicano identity from knowledge of the bleaker aspects of the past, might have exposed us to religion not only as the majestic and uniting force that it was in ancient Mexico, but as an oppressive force as well. In the Amerindian theocracy, religion was omnipresent in all manifestations of life, usually regulating war, the seeding of crops, and even amusement and recreation. The amerindios concentrated on spiritual methods to meet the challenges of life rather than on mechanical methods. They used mixtures of magic and religion to obtain good crops, long life, health, wealth, prestige, children, and happiness. Phrases and formulas, divinations, rites and ceremonies, all were used to placate, assist, or force the deities into action. Many Mexican gods were conceived in the image of men and women with all their perfections and imperfections, with capacity for friendship and for hatred, with passions and desires. Such gods could be wheedled, propitiated, and gratified with presents. In return they could be benevolent, helpful, and generous to el indio. But they could also be offended or insulted and could inflict countless calamities, including drought, famine, flood, hurricane, lightning, sickness, misery, and death. A great section of Indian society was dedicated to discovering the desires of the gods, propitiating their enmities, and obtaining fulfillment of the desires of the people.

The matter of symbolic destruction, or human sacrifice, has been one of profound concern and ambivalence in both Mexican intellectual and popular thought, but as yet it has barely been given play by Chicanos, even those who have cultivated the pre-Columbian roots. It is excruciatingly difficult to genuinely maintain objectivity about lo indio in this regard. I remember vividly the pendulations of San Diego/Tijuana society during my youth. As I recollect, in the late 1940s and early 1950s the facts of human sacrifice on the part of the Aztecs and other amerindios were mostly denied by official or semi-official opinion makers (newspapers, magazines, cinema noticieros, etc.) and by many educated persons who should have been less swayed by their belief that the pre-Columbian cultures represented a level of civilized perfection untainted by systemic cruelties or by the development from barbarie to civilización that so many cultures have undergone. Hardline denials only gradually softened over many years to a more objective understanding. On the other end of the pendulum were the cynical naysayers, Mexicans who considered themselves purely European racially and culturally and for whom lo indio was the epitome of all that was backward in Mexico. (When I used to attend the Tijuana Jai Alai where my brother played professionally, there was a player whom I suppose on the basis of observable physical characteristics was Mexican Indian and stood out markedly from his Basque peers, the Solozábales, Urquiagas, and Mendiolas. Whenever he missed a play, the crowd, which was also Mexican, would taunt him harder than any other and with special jeers such as "Indio Triste," "Macario," "Indito de Lerdo Chiquito," and the like).

Although human sacrifice seems cruel and horrible and indefensible to most laypersons, the trained anthropologist knows that this practice is a step that many peoples have taken, all over the world, on the road to civilization. It was practiced at some period in Africa, Asia, Australia, Alaska, South America, and Europe. Human sacrifice presupposes an organization of complex relationships in which the ritual of sacrifice plays the important part of tying together the social, economic, political, and religious ideas and institutions and symbolizes the acceptance on the part of the human race of responsibilities for events formerly thought to be beyond its control.

Similarly, Alurista as anthropologist could have but didn't evoke the social hierarchy of the indigenista military theocracy, which was characterized by castes with hereditary power. Alonso de Zurita names four classes of nobility: Tlaloques, lords with civil and criminal jurisdiction and governors of provinces; Tectecuhtzin, the ubiquitous feudal landowners-for-life who seem to appear in every society, with serfs to work their lands; Calpullec, oldest relatives or heads of families, that is, free farmers, workers of land held by the calpulli or clans; and finally, Pipiltzin, the sons of nobles, who were free of tribute. On the bottom rung of the Aztec social ladder were the slaves. They were usually taken in warfare, but many people who incurred unpayable debts or were sentenced for crimes entered into slavery. Slaves could marry and have free children and could also possess slaves. A slave could regain his freedom by raising the sum for which he had been bought. By the time the Spanish invaded, the Aztecs had a complicated and highly stratified society which categorized many levels of nobles, commoners, and slaves. Indeed, Moctezuma, the Aztec ruler when the Spanish arrived, was losing contact with his people because of the tremendous personal prestige, self-divinization, elaborate ceremonials, and rigid court etiquette that elevated him high above even the nobility. An ordinary person did not dare look him in the face, and high officials had to change their elaborate dress for common clothes before each interview with him.

GARY D. KELLER

The role of women in pre-Columbian society is not one that the modern Chicana is apt to look upon with great satisfaction, although it should be noted that Amerindian gods were typically dualistic. All things were based on male and female elements that gave birth to the gods, to the world, and to the human race. Women were permitted into certain priesthoods because of this dualistic cosmogeny, and female priests called Cihuateopixque flourished in Mexico, although not much is known of them (the chroniclers having been exclusively male?). The women priests had charge of the education of girls and they sometimes had special cults like the priestesses called Cihuacuacuilli, dedicated to the earth goddess. All this aside, some thinkers have proposed that the machismo of the Spaniard and of the Amerindian combined in some exponential fashion to produce a sort of cultural *aqua regia*, intensifying the worst of both chauvinisms in Mexico. ¡Y mira el resultado! Chicana feminists are mostly still involved with breast-beating lamentations of the pinche malinche variety (it is curious how many Chicana poems rhyme these two words), but that is beginning to change. Sylvia Morales, director and scriptwriter of the recent, notable film *Chicana*, reviews the role of woman in pre-Columbian society and finds her to be the military, religious, and socioeconomic pawn of the Amerindian patriarchy. The vision of Amerindia that is offered by Alurista is not likely to be totally acceptable to the Chicana feminist inasmuch as it does not pursue indio male chauvinism and domination.

In addition, as Ybarra-Frausto has observed, the poetic anthropology of Alurista does not take into account the relationship between indios and chicanos in contemporary USA. It would appear to incorporate lo indio into chicanismo in one fell swoop, but a deep examination of the implications of this "unity" would certainly lead to the conclusion that this incorporation papers over great historical, ethnic, and social differences, and often, antagonisms.

One final observation must be made in connection with both the veracity and the efficacy of Alurista's Amerindian anthropological poetic. This refers to the historical circumstances of the Alurista texts themselves. Our poet cultivated the theme of Aztlán and other Mesoamerican motifs during what is now often called the "tumultuous" phase of Chicano literature. It can be argued, and I believe with some legitimacy, that this was a period that did not admit intensive self-criticism or vacilations, peros, emperos, and reparos. The Chicano consciousness as it related to Aztlán, to Amerindia, was embryonic and emergent. In short, we were in a period of consciousness-formation and consciousness-raising and not of refinement or qualification. Such refinement and adjustment is for a subsequent period. Alurista, it could be argued, was "right" in injecting a good dose of ethnic pride into Chicano self-understanding even at the expense of a less than comprehensive anthropology. Similarly, the social and political context of *Floricanto* and *Nationchild* themselves determined this ordering of thematic motifs. In short, even if Alurista had thought to do otherwise, the social and political context would have made it very difficult for him to establish more than basic, overt contrasts between an idyllic Amerindia and a ruthless Anglo-America.

Just as Alurista has asked for certain modifications in the textual appearance of *Nationchild plumaroja* in this second edition which perhaps reflect or befit the 1980s, let me then offer the polemical considerations of his poetic that I have surveyed as well as some observations about the seamier side of Amerindia, in a spirit which gives due and sympathetic consideration to Alurista's "tumultuous" genesis of Aztlán in the 70s while at the same time placing his poems in a contratextual relationship that takes into account a firmer and more self-confident Chicano identity in the 80s, one whose appetite is whetted by an evaluation of internal or historical Raza conflicts and contradictions and by the literary epiphenomena that may have resulted from these frictions and fractions.

As our poet has received recognition and invitations to travel around the United States and even abroad, his themes have become cross-cultural. Here too the perceptions are romantic. Alurista, the poet himself, and la cultura chicana are the templates against which other peoples and cultures are observed and measured. For example, several of the poems in *Dawn's Eye* treat the Netherlands, particularly the city of Amsterdam, on the occasion of Alurista's trip to Europe at the invitation of the Dutch. References to this novel experience abound in the poems:

GARY D. KELLER

> cross the chino snow the vikings listen to the mayanano,
> nano, parked above the roof. lofty bleeding without
> bogart, cagney or pacino. alive. haciendo la lucha
>
> ("People Asking Me")

In "Nether, Nether, Netherland" we find counterposed the stereotypical expectations of the naive poet experiencing a new culture for the first time,

> viking cliffs kirk douglas hath no horns upon his casket,

(a reference to the Hollywood movie, *The Vikings*), with the actual presence of the country in its concrete details:

> nether, nether, netherland coffee cups imported from
> taiwan and main china marbles slung against the windmills
> they slinged shot rhythm upon the wooden gliders off the
> viking cliffs . . .

Equally counterposed in this poem (and at the same time tied together by the historical facts of the slave trade) are the impressions of the Lowlands and those of the península yucateca, the huracanes of the Gulf of Mexico and the Caribbean Sea, and the Mexican state of Chiapas.

In the long, superb poem, "From Amsterdam" we find our poet alternately astonished by Hispania in the Dutch city,

> no lo creo todavía
> debo estar soñando,
> hablando en español
> escuchando a silvio rodríguez
> en casa de arie
> en amsterdam

touched by the culture of Amsterdam and the concern for all peoples that he finds there,

> en realidad es un mundo sólo
> sólo uno y somos todos humanos
> y nos duele lo mismo a todos
> a rembrandt lo enterraron
> aquí y aquí anne frank hizo
> su diario tito puente toca
> hoy en la noche mientras
> el cuarto tribunal bertrand

> russell enfoca con su lupa
> holandesa sobre los derechos
> de los pueblos amerindios

and also profoundly offended by the racism that is so universally
pervasive among the human race:

> me miran como turco,
> suriname o indonesio
> cuando bien soy amerindio
> chicano moro maya con
> salsa de país vasco los
> taxis no me hacen caso
> y me empapo en el
> racismo de holanda
> ni las prostitutas nos
> ofrecen sus ombligos
> no parecemos turistas
> víctor, pedro y yo

Ultimately, in this matrix of contradictory feelings and cross-
cultural perceptions it is the novelty, the "debo estar soñando"
quality of his presence in Europe ("ayer salió mi foto en el periódico nacional / hoy no salgo a la calle") which affects Alurista most,
as well as his Chicano readers. How satisfying and liberating it
is really to be abroad with our laureado Chicano poet experiencing with him his agridulce, amorodio impressions. To be recognized and taken seriously, both the poet and his Raza readership,
to feel, aquí en Europa, aquí en nether, netherland, that we can
send USA to the deuce! Once again our cross-culturalist vuelve
a su raza with his quandry and the riddle of these novel feelings for
us to jointly solve:

> . . . ¿será la pólvora
> en el aire? ¿será yin-yang?
> los espermatozoides "y"
> nadan mejor que los
> "x" cuyo vigor es menor
> habrá que preguntar
> al maestro anaya tal
> vez hinojosa sabe sin
> embargo ruíz y esparza
> han capturado la luz

>   tal vez ellos me saquen
>   de este apuro . . .

Dawn's Eye is not merely a contrast and comparison between Aztlán/USA and the Lowlands. In a procedure analogous to his appropriation of a swath of languages in order to mold his own multilingual poetic persona, Alurista, in his newest book of poems, co-opts a wide range of peoples in order to produce a literary universe that is rich and dense in cross-cultural reverberations. The culture and language of both the insular boricua ("Eran, He Ran") as well as the hip Spanish Harlemite ("Subway No Way") are evoked. As is characteristic of Alurista's poetry, black lingo, particularly with respect to jazz and blues, is well represented. There are emulations of calypso ("Fire and Earth"), references to Spain and especially to the poet's Basque roots ("Azucena"), references to the moros and the moriscos (not to mention the mariscos!) in "Then It Is a Prison," references to the Palestinians ("This Ol' World") and to Eastern culture and religion ("People Asking Me"). Moreover, *Dawn's Eye* is also a personal archaeo-anthropology. Many of the poems are devoted to aspects of the poet's family life, particularly relaciones matrimoniales, and the first two poignant poems in the collection are moving eulogies to the poet's father. Here again the cross-cultural allusion works wonderfully. Taking from Amerindia, from España, and from Aztlán, combining lo divino y lo profano, the chivalric and the quixotesque, recreating the handing down of a Chicano motocicleta genio from pater noster to his adoring son, Alurista creates in "Baltazar" a snapshot worthy of Vasconcelos' raza cósmica:

>   yo te conocí
>   a los diez años
>   con todo el genio
>   que tú ofrecías
>   padre
>   y tu motocicleta
>   en mil novecientos
>   cincuenta y siete
>   sorteando
>   molinos de maíz

Alurista's Poetics

Tomás Ybarra-Frausto, in a notably fertile paper, has defined Alurista's poetics in terms of its oral, bilingual and pre-Colombian qualities. Under the conceptual rubric "oral," Ybarra-Frausto identifies what are perhaps two strands: the element of public performance and the ritual element. According to the critic,

> . . . Alurista has helped establish another significant dimension of contemporary Chicano poetry: the emphasis on poetry as spoken rather than privately read. The Chicano poet writes for an audience that is not predominantly a reading audience, and on the whole has little inclination to value the printed word. This public's educational level does not predispose it to habitual reading, especially of poetry. Chicano poets assume that their audience will not ponder individual lines, savoring the formal composition by reading and rereading. A Chicano audience is more likely to hear the poem, perhaps only once, and must comprehend it as it is sung or spoken. This focus on public comprehension calls for rhythmic patterning, a strong narrative line and frequent use of the vernacular to reverse the tradition of private poets who elaborate a personal hermetic world in their verse. Alurista by contrast stresses the communal nature of poetry with an outward social thrust.[14]

I believe that Ybarra has overstated the case for Alurista's immediate public accessibility.[15] On the one hand, it would appear that he represents Alurista as a poet who had an intensive following among the lowest socioeconomic sector of Raza society, barrio batos as it were, the proletariado and even the subproletariado. I doubt the accuracy of that assumption. An evaluation of Alurista's scholarly credentials as stated in his curriculum vitae reveals that he has recited much more frequently in academic settings than anywhere else. For example, between 1968 and 1974 Alurista recited or lectured at 41 universities and community colleges, including the major intellectual centers of California, Texas, Colorado, Arizona, Michigan, and elsewhere. He recited at eight literary festivals and gatherings (clearly intellectual types of meetings) such as the Symposium on Latin American/Chicano literature in San Diego and the Quinto Festival de Teatros Chicanos y Primer Encuentro Latinoamericano in Mexico City. He records only two recitals that we would remotely associate with barrio or genuinely proletarian Raza society: at the California

Rehabilitation Center and the Tehachepi State Prison. On the basis of where Alurista has been invited and where he has indicated he has recited, his readership and audience would appear to be if not of a middle-class background socioeconomically, to certainly have group aspirations that we would associate with that class and also the intellectual discipline and education to read and comprehend sophisticated poetry. Second, while we should not deny that several of Alurista's poems have qualities of public performance and easy accessibility on the basis of listening rather than reading, the concept of "the oral" is capable of being overemphasized as an analytic vehicle for interpreting the written texts as gathered into the first two collections, *Floricanto* and *Nationchild*. In addition, it should be mentioned that the concept of orality becomes less useful and somewhat out of date with respect to the works published after Ybarra's paper (1979), *A'nque, Spik in Glyph?* and *Dawn's Eye*.

Within the work that concerns us the most, *Nationchild*, there are a number of poems that are addressed directly to la Raza, for example, "Carnales el amor nos pertenece," "Let Yourself Be Sidetracked by Your Güiro," "Because la Raza is Tired," "Through the Fences that Surround You, Grita," "Come Down My Cheek Raza Roja," and many others. These poems, particularly, have public performance qualities and surely have been at the core of Alurista's repertoire when reciting before the public. However, even the most "oral" poems—in the sense Ybarra-Frausto has described them—have qualities identical to those that predominate in the later books. For example, the first poem in *Nationchild* cultivates the theme of death in a markedly erudite fashion,

> no iré a mi entierro
>> my epitaph will be blank in my solace
>>> ("We Would Have Been Relieved With Death")

and the second poem, "Salsa Con Crackers," despite the promising orality of the title, is replete with recondite language and a liberal use of educated alliteration,

> prelogical fruit
>> prehistorical experience entre las palmas
> entrando a preprimaria

Another example, "I Like to Sleep," already makes use of the Aluristian "glyph," which is later elaborated in *Spik in Glyph?* This visual array genuinely requires a reading of the printed version for real understanding:

```
of success, of co in
              co opt
              cut out
                sp
                     lit
                        go
                           n
                             e
y el bato likes heavy dreams
```

Moreover, in the same collection (*Nationchild*) there appears the sort of highly literary, personal (as opposed to communal), and meditative poem represented by "I Have Found My Flesh,"

> henceforth i can only do but that which the assertion
> of my self implies in the form of a must. little less
> puede resultar ante al encuentro accidental con la muerte
> forging the skeleton of its structure into a mobile

Pardon our "henceforths," but this poem probably never had nor was intended to have the benefit of public recitation.

The point that needs to be emphasized is that while much of the earlier poetry of Alurista—like "Corky" Gonzales' *Yo Soy Joaquín*—was unmistakably suited for public recitation (although not necessarily for a proletarian public[16]), Alurista should not be converted into the poet analog of Luis Valdez and his correligionarios, who created the *actos* on agitprop models for the avowed purpose of influencing the farmworkers to union action.

Alurista's poetry may have influenced some of el grueso público, but it should be recognized that his work, even at its most hortative, is rich in nuances, metaphors, bilingual double entendres, word plays, and figures of speech that require a certain sensitivity to Náhuatl and Maya poetry, all of which dampen any direct appeal to the urban or agricultural worker in the manner of El Teatro Campesino. Second, Alurista's own putative goals for el pueblo have been rather complex; this has resulted, with respect to social action, in his creating a center called Toltecas en

Aztlán, where "cultural guerrillas" were to be trained in the study of pre-Columbian and Chicano art, music, literature, science, and philosophy, and, subsequently, his establishment of a group named "Servidores al Arbol de la Vida," which as Ybarra-Frausto points out:

> . . . attempted to re-create Indian chant and ritual singing and dance forms in a modern context. While maintaining a reverent attitude toward the spiritual intent of their performance, they wove a secular sociopolitical commentary into their texts. A key assumption in many of these song-poems is that spiritual and material realities must be fused . . .[17]

Finally, much of Alurista's appeal as a performing poet stems from his charismatic qualities (of interest here perhaps is the fact that he has worked as a group counselor, psychiatric childcare worker, and psychology instructor) and hypnotic rhythms, in short, his strong personal appeal as a performer. Alurista's charisma is not unlike Allen Ginsberg's, who in Anglo society influenced a broad although educated and non-proletarian sector of youths and adults. Alurista finds Ginsberg appealing himself, and refers to him in "From Amsterdam,"

> y el zen ginsberg me
> cayó muy bien, personal-
> mente, digo 'ora que ...
> podíamos platicar sobre
> su obra . . .

Indeed, the performance analogy between Ginsberg and Alurista brings us to the second strand that Ybarra-Frausto identifies in our poet's orality: the religious and ritual element. Ybarra-Frausto refers to an interview with Alurista where the poet recalls standing on a hill and watching the long line of farmworkers and supporters as they walked the asphalt highway chanting and singing, led by fluttering red and black thunderbird flags with images of the Virgin of Guadalupe held aloft.

> It was the farmworkers who brought Chicanos to the forefront of national consciousness. As I watched the pilgrimage from Delano, I said to myself, that man Chávez is either a fool, a fanatic or a truly wise man. And very soon his genius was apparent.[18]

However, while Alurista may have recognized the genius of Chávez—including the genius of combining spiritual and mythic impulses with socioeconomic, political, and ideological goals—he did not follow the philosophy of the farmworkers as articulated in the *Plan de Delano*, which incorporates traditional Catholicism into a social philosophy of non-violent revolution, universal brotherhood, social action, pilgrimage, and penitence. Alurista's religious themes in his poetry, as well as the esthetic of ritual which marks some of his verse—here both fondo and forma are consonant—lean toward the pre-Columbian rather than the Christian. This is another prominent feature of our poet that leads him away from, say, a communal or consensual relationship with the great Chicano público such as that which the early Luis Valdez can properly be claimed to have enjoyed. Alurista instead directs himself toward that personally fulfilling goal of recuperating the pre-Columbian Chicano underpinnings.

In Alurista's poetry there are abundant religious allusions as well as references to the Church, but the religion is more often than not pre-Columbian and, moreover, when Catholicism is referred to it is not typically in a flattering manner. Although examples could be drawn from most of Alurista's works, they are especially prevalent in *Nationchild*. In "When You Have the Earth in Mouthful," Padre Hidalgo is justified as a decidedly extra-clerical cleric:

> . . . dentro de la campana que
> repica hidalgo — fuera de la iglesia
> el padre clama justicia, libertad y
> tierra. dentro de ella nunca existió
> dicho sueño — no pa'l pueblo, no pa' la
> raza, pa' la gente; pa' nosotros
> nada. "ni ma' carnal" me dice
> el bato; "se acabó la onda." i don't
> understand that kind of payasadas.
> con mi gente no se juega . . .

The poem closes in an iconoclastic manner:

> we got our razared
>   we got our barro
> we don't need your "holy" breath

"Cuando la cucaracha camine" presents the cucaracha as a crucified symbol of liberty and the poet as a "little altar boy" who hasn't been told the truth. It closes on a

> chicano mass
> to preach about the kingdom of man and woman
> (god has been ruler long enough as god)
> men and women have to learn themselves about
> one another, to love each other
> (chicanos will then preach of the kingdom of god)

In "Nuestra Casa — Denver '69" the poet calls for

> no more rezos de rodillas
> no more apologies por ser de carne
> y de hueso . . .

"Candle Shuffle" is particularly virulent and left-leaning. It glosses a venal obispo who,

> covered in black robe
> con cruz
> pendiente al ombligo
> carga la
> crucifixión en la panza llena
> de sermones about
> heavenly kingdoms for
> the working poor
> who are meek
> and give tithe
> "¡10% pa'l señor!"
> ¿cuál señor?
> ¡el señor sacerdote!
> ¡la señora iglesia!
> "el cielo!! el cielo!!
> that never gave us posada

One should not think that all of Alurista's snipes at Catholicism are of the solemn or bombastic type. In "Construyendo una balsa" he evokes the Don Juan myth of repayment for sin in an amusing manner, having Death dine on tortillas.

> it is then no surprise or misguided expectation that
> materializes itself in the form of calavera romántica
> que cena con la muerte, tortilla en mano and entirely
> committed to the act of being . . .

Occasionally separated from the vision of a corrupted Church and clergy are aspects of the Christian mythopoesis which are syncretistically combined with pre-Columbian lore. The birth of la Raza is juxtaposed several times in Alurista's poetry with el nacimiento de Cristo. One of the most moving examples is in "Come Down My Cheek Raza Roja," where a "possible nacimiento" is prefigured halfway through the poem. Indeed the poem closes in the following manner:

> cultivate el maíz de nuestra
> identidad indígena
> a la vida, a la muerte
> al nacimiento de un nopal

Another clear example is in "A Child To Be Born." Again the Christ-child is la Raza, Aztlán:

> a child to be born
>   pregnant is the continente
> el barro y la raza
>   to bear aztlán on our forehead

Instead of wise men or kings being led to the manger,

> . . . the crickets call the birth
>   and the ranas arrullan al nacido
> y las víboras del mar siguen a la campanita . . .

Indeed, this syncretic confluence of religions is prefigured by and is one of the keys to understanding the title of the work itself, *Nationchild plumaroja*. For the title evokes not only linguistic, ideological, mythic, racial, ethnic, and historical elements in the poems, but religious and ritualistic ones as well. The child that is born—or rather, in the anthropological poetic of Alurista, reborn or recovered—is a Christ/Quetzalcóatl/Kukulkán[19] child, a child-nation of quintessential religious significance. In this context it is entirely fitting that Alurista should inform us that our pueblo is deific (in "Tal vez porque te quiero"),

> raza mía
> molten bronze unto a god
>   chicano-hermano, hermana chicana
> derretido en las llamas
>   razasol

that our people were born of cataclysmic fire,

> they who crawl and fly al fuego se lanzaron
> la serpiente emplumada se hizo sol y el cascabel ...
> el cascabel en víbora prendido
> comenzó la música que hizo al pueblo de fuego.
>> ("Before the Flesh in Bones")

that the older, more profound verities underlie the Christian mythopoesis,

> dile que dios no es de lata, de fierro
> ni de aluminio
> dile que dios es de bronce
> que guadalupe es tonantzin
> y que san pedro es chicano
>> ("Tata Juan")

that la Raza lives not only under the charitable = passive Christian teachings,

> learn to live without
> asking your god
> to be kind, gentle
> and to change . . .
>> ("Face Your Fears Carnal")

and finally that Aztlán is a multicultural, multilingual confluence, but one where the Amerindian deities take absolute precedence:

> aztlán, aztlán
> the semilla que plantó nuestro padre quetzalcóatl
> ya germina
> en el vientre de nuestra
> madrecontinentetierra, amerindia
> nationchild de su padrecarnalismo kukulcán
>> ("A Child To Be Born")

In Alurista's poetry the religious content is cemented together by the ritual empaque. Indeed, Alurista has been the guiding genius behind the creation of the Festivales de Flor y Canto, and these in turn evoke the devotion that Amerindia had to music, song, and dance from the earliest times in ancient Mexico, but especially during the Classic period. The Aluristian Festival de Flor y Canto evokes, from the point of view of social structure, the special academies of song and dance that existed in Mexico during pre-Hispanic times, the Cuicacalli or Mixcoacalli (House of Song), and from the perspective of worship, the Mesoamerican gods Xochipilli (Flower Prince), god of games, song, dance, mimicry, plastic arts, palace courtiers, and the ubiquitous ball games; and Huehuecoyotl (Reverend Old Coyote), the god in charge of song.

Music in ancient Mexico had the principal function of supporting religious ceremonies, providing a background of rhythm, movement, and action for community participation. Music for recreation was probably not so important in the pre-Hispanic social pattern as it is to us today. An additional function was military: music was used to scare off the enemy or confuse him in the heat of battle by the continuous blowing of trumpets and whistles. Mesoamerican songs told of ancient traditions or remote deeds of the clans, of their deities, wars, victories, feats of famous warriors, outstanding news events such as comets and earthquakes, death, famine, love, humor, hunting incidents, illnesses, plagues, the enemy, and the afterworlds. In this way much of the history of the people was spread and perpetuated. The Spanish tried to extinguish this custom. Frederick Peterson cites an order of 1555 that categorically states:

> The Indians shall not sing the said chants of their rites or ancient histories, without first having the said chants examined by the Clergy, or by people that understand the language very well. The ministers of the Gospel shall see that there is nothing of profane things in such chants.[20]

As religion was inextricably linked with singing, dancing, and instrumentation, the people could not make any music that was not connected with "profane things." Peterson judges that,

> It took a long time to extinguish pure pre-hispanic singing and dancing, but the old customs were sabotaged by substituting Christian arrangements under strict supervision. The pre-hispanic community participation in singing and dancing was persecuted by Spanish religious and political officials. One of the great evils wrought by the Spanish in Mexico was the disruption of most aspects of community participation. This was manifested in the instruments which they brought with them, and the use to which they put them. They were used to giving solo performances before audiences of non-participants or to playing for their own sol-

itary pleasure. The Spanish favoured stringed instruments of the lute type, from which the guitar evolved, for solitary playing. So the sale by Spanish merchants of these stringed instruments to the Indians indicated breakdown of communal aspects of native music.[21]

Alurista has very clearly noted the communal nature of song and dance in pre-Columbian society participated in by every person in the community who was not infirm or feeble. The rulers, nobility, priests, officials, merchants, school children, fathers and mothers, and grandparents all danced together. In one of his articles on esthetics, both his own and of ancient Mexico, he observes:

> We should note that in contrast to European poetry written by the privileged classes and destined for the same audience, Nahuatl poetry was publicly sung, dialogued, and collectively danced as much by the nobility as by the working classes. And although much of it was written in elevated style with didactic intent, it never ceased being an object of tribal recreation and delight.[22]

What in Amerindia was communal and religious, and contrastive to the European esthetic that ultimately suppressed its existence, is transformed in Alurista's Chicano artistic manifesto. It becomes both communal and emphatically class and ethnic conscious (as well as religion sensitive, except that religion serves to enhance radical ideology) and equally contrastive to the Western—e.g., Anglo-American—esthetic.

Not only is the ideology of ritual (which is also a ritual of ideology) examined by Alurista, his basic goal being to transpose Amerindian ritual communion and update it for Chicano poetico-political life, but our poeta-antropólogo also chooses to cultivate ritual genre. Both *Floricanto* and *Nationchild* use the genre of cantos. *Nationchild* further refines the pre-Columbian esthetic by dividing the cantos into five Mayan *katunes* (units of 20) using the symbols of animals or flowers—nopal, xochitl (flower), serpiente, conejo, venado—to signify a particular type of energía or mood. In *Timespace* the ritual genre of verse is present in the fifteen opening tunas alabanzas and in the canciones crepúsculos, the décimas meditaciones, the ojos de dios, the songs for dawn, and so on. Finally, *A'nque* once again is composed of canciones and cantos as well as a few cuentos. Only the last two collections,

Spik in Glyph? and *Dawn's Eye*, break with the overarching, circumscribing genre of ritual verse.

Another facet of Alurista's goal of applying ritual and religion in the quest of both spiritual and ethnic/class consciousness-raising has been his use of ceremony and spectacle. Ybarra-Frausto has suggested Alurista's ideal as being "to bring composition and performance together in a single improvised event."[23] Elsewhere he terms Alurista a "songman" who recognizes "the physical basis of the poem within him. The articulation of sound springs from the imagination, creating the lines of the poem in direct relation to breath patterns."[24] During the period of vigencia of the Servidores del Arbol de la Vida, Alurista, with Juan Felipe Herrera and Mario Aguilar, created an ensemble which attempted to recuperate Indian song, chant, and ritual dancing within a modern context. The parameters of this effort were to combine a respectful rendition of the original material, particularly with regard to its spiritual elements, while at the same time weaving radical Chicano sociopolitical commentary into the texts. Ybarra-Frausto describes our poet "playing the conch, a modern adaptation of a pre-Conquest instrument and experimenting with sound," developing "a style of recitation which is a cross between Gregorian chant and monotone," and attempting to create a "poetry not only in the mind but also in the viscera."[25]

As a performer Alurista has no peer among Chicano poets. His popularity has been for the Chicano community on a par with Allen Ginsberg's for the Anglo world.

Alurista's Stylistic Multilingualism

One of the most notable characteristics of Alurista's poetry is its multilingualism (we have already touched upon his bicultural and cross-cultural qualities). Alurista's appropriation of language, apparently both in everyday usage and for creative purposes, is deliberately expansive. In his interview with Bruce-Novoa he responded to a question about his own language use at home with an observation that highlighted a deliberate expansion of registers *within* languages as well as code-switching between English and Spanish:

As for my own family, in my house Spanish and English are spoken.

> I speak bilingually and I do it very deliberately when I speak to
> my son, who can now understand me. I speak to him in English
> and in Spanish; I speak to him in Chicano Spanish and Mexican
> Spanish; I speak to him in Yankee English and sometimes I even
> throw him a little Black English, so that he'll get into it. He's got
> to be hip; he's got to know what's happening. . . . As far as I'm
> concerned, he ought to know at least one form of Spanish and
> one form of English well, so he can communicate with anyone;
> that is, with Chicanos and Chicanas, as well as non-Spanish speak-
> ers.[26]

In another study I have shown how it is common that once a
writer has made the decision "to create literary texts in a bilingual
medium, that this decision leads to added sensitivity to the levels
of register within language. Thus *interlinguistic* literary texts lead
naturally to a richer *intralinguistic* expressivity."[27] As I shall show
subsequently, Alurista provides a clear example of this enriching
phenomenon. Alurista himself was alert to his multilingual stylistic
and is properly proud of his pioneering role.

> I don't want to brag, but I believe that I was the first modern
> Chicano writer who dared send bilingual work to an editor. I re-
> member the reaction of one editor when I first gave him my poetry.
> He said, "Listen, this is a pochismo. Why can't you write either in
> Spanish or in English?" Or, "This doesn't look very good, and
> what's all this Black English you put here? You ought to use correct
> English. And all of these vatoisms or chicanoisms; that doesn't
> sound good; it's the decadence of our Spanish language." I told
> him, "Look, I am a writer and a poet. If you like it, publish it; and
> if not, don't fuck with me, leave me in peace." He said he wouldn't
> publish trash like that when I first talked to him. However, a week
> later he called me on the telephone and said, "Send me your work
> because it's going to be a big hit." So I sent him the work he want-
> ed. I sent him about thirty pieces, out of which he published ten.
> After that, if I'm not mistaken, many Chicano and Chicana writers
> began to publish bilingually.[28]

To Bruce-Novoa's question about whether or not Chicano
literature has a particular language or idiom, Alurista responded
in a fashion that sheds great light on his own use of language for
poetic purposes.

> What truly makes chicano literature so rich and fertile is the fact
> that we can and do in fact write in Black English and Yankee
> English, in Mexican Spanish and Chicano Spanish. Many of us
> are beginning to restore or bring to life, some of the indigenous

languages, such as Mayan and Nahuatl. I try to do this in most of my work, at least the work published to date. I use six languages: Black English, Anglo English, Mexican Spanish, Chicano Spanish, Nahuatl, and Maya. So I really don't think there is a particular language in Chicano literature. We cover this full range in Chicano literature, the full range of colors, the full rainbow. All of the sarape. It is one great sauce and that makes it all the tastier, don't you think? That shows our versatility and multidimensional view of the world. That makes us stronger, a broadly based, more universal people. And as writers, that puts us in a completely different category in the history of world literature.[29]

For Alurista, his use of language is another way of being revolutionary. No mind that his claim for Chicano literature generally that it is multilingual is an allegation that doesn't fit many Raza writers. Nor should we overly concern ourselves with the fact that other literatures have utilized this mode as well and prior to Chicano literature,[30] so that we can't quite put ourselves "in a completely different category in the history of world literature." (After all, what is entirely new under the Fifth Sun!) The most pertinent point relates to Alurista's linguistic expansionism itself as an enriching and reverberating poetic alternative to common communication.

Let us begin with the common Word. Ordinary language primarily serves a social purpose and it does so by codifying those aspects of reality that a society wishes to control. Language can be regarded as a socially sanctioned representation of the external world. Without such a representation the external world is a chaos beyond human control. The members of a society accept the codification their language provides because it gives them a necessary sense of security; reality is under control because they share a common means of communication. Communication can only take place if there are conventionally accepted ways of looking at the world. What Alurista's work does by its use of, among other resources, a multilingual mode as well as a variety of registers within each language is to surpass the conventionally recognized languages of Anglos, of Blacks, of Latin-Americans, even of Chicanos themselves, even though the latter use a bilingual medium. He develops a polyglot poetry charged with ideological and religious implications which takes from English, from Spanish, from Amerindian languages, but which in its artistic integration of each of these elements transcends them as mere instruments of communal intercourse and renders them into a polyphonic voice that is genuinely unique.

Of all our poets perhaps Alurista has been the most deliberately mindful of multilingualism. His use of English takes command of registers such as the Black variety that he refers to in his interview as well as the high oratorical dialect and, of course, the more middle-class, quotidian tongue.

In *Dawn's Eye* ("Penetra") he reproduces English language crooning,

> xoo b do b do, clink clink, tom tom
> xoo b do b do tom tom, clink clink
> xoo b do b do tom clink, clink tom
> radio gonna sing all night, u know?

as well as popular song ("Mama Don't Want U"),

> "mama don't want u
>   dadi don't need u
>   momi cain't buy u love—"

He also arrogates to himself the orthodox register of solemn and serious Poetry:

> sliver
> moondrum
>   silence
> cross the desert
>   dusk of
>   sweeping hawks
>   solitude remains
>   ("Sliver")

Moreover, and I have cited this example earlier from *Nationchild*, he is capable of consciously recreating the archaic or the Victorian to poetic advantage:

> henceforth i can only do but that which the assertion
> of my self implies in the form of a must . . .

With respect to Spanish, a similar polyphony is apparent. He can write in a high oratorical Spanish as he does in *Timespace huracán,*

> independencia y libertad
> cadenas rotas
>   la raza libre sobre
>   la tierra
>   camina en busca
>   de nuestra nación
>   ("Cadenas rotas")

or he can begin in that same high register and then switch intra-linguistically to a Chicano or popular *mexicano* locution,

> a pelear
>   en la tierra
>   contra los pueblos
>   que conocen
>   lo mero principal
>   ("A pelear")

Alurista's *dominio* over Mexican Spanish is more extensive than many other Raza poets, permitting him to sprinkle his poetry with effects or *picardías* that are not much known north of the border:

> no tenemos espada
> tampoco
> tampico
>   (" 'Apá," *Dawn's Eye*)
> y te dicen batman—Yankee sacón!
>   ("Criollo You Lived Prohibition," *Nationchild*)

With the use of Amerindian languages Alurista is in a radically different circumstance. In his cultivation of English and of Spanish he can count on a bilingual readership. His Spanish-English bilinguals, however, are unfamiliar with Náhuatl or Maya. Elsewhere[31] I have described the techniques that Ernest Hemingway utilized to evoke the Spanish language for a monolingual, English-speaking readership. Alurista's challenge is similar. The manner in which he has met it has been at least fourfold:

(1) He has never overwhelmed the reader with Amerindian language, preferring to introduce a sprinkling of Náhuatl or Maya into a poem where the base text is in English or an alternation of

both of these Western tongues. Moreover, the utilization of Amerindian has not necessarily been for conceptual or intellectual purposes, but more to evoke the flavor of lo indio, particularly the ritualistic quality of Amerindian poetry,

> relación / rama / raíz
> nación / ama / maíz
> maiztlán chilam balam
> maiztlán tonan é tollan
> teotihuacán / tihuanaco / tepoztlán
>
> ("Luna llena," *Timespace huracán*)

or for rhythmic patterning

> mismaló ya
> mismaloyá
> sá lamandra mís maloya
> salá mandra mismá loya
> salamán dra mismaló ya
> salamandrá mismaloyá
>
> ("Trópico de ceviche," *Nationchild*)

(2) When engaged in utilizing Amerindian for conceptual or intellectual reasons, Alurista has typically introduced simple words rather than syntactical chunks. The words reflect either deities or personages who are generally known,

> back to the tears of tlaloc's agony ("Eternal Tripas")
> ojos rojos de coraje en plumas de quetzal ("Piedra roca niebla")
> el de cuauhtémoc, tizoc
> o el plumado moctezuma ("Tuning Flower Tones")

and they often serve to introduce the less known,

> ollintonatiuh, back to aztlán ("Eternal tripas")
> look at tonantzín ("Chalice")

or objects:

> i found a calpulli [= clan] ("A través de los sueños")
> papalotl papalotl al sol ya vuelas [= kite] ("Madre tumba soledad")

(3) Alurista, as we have described earlier, has been engaged

in an educational plan of action, attempting to teach Amerindian philosophy, culture, and so on, to la Raza.

(4) Our poet has also formed bilingual, English-Spanish portmanteau words such as Pepsicóatl and Cocacóatl (in his play *Dawn*).

Another element in Alurista's introduction of Amerindian language into the Chicano consciousness through his poetry is more indirect. It involves the use of Spanish words, some of them fairly esoteric, others common, which have Amerindian origins. For example, Alurista often utilizes the following: milpa, nopal, jacal, tuna, xochitl, colibrí, maguey, atole, and comal.

Egla Morales Blouin[32] has shown how Alurista and other Chicano poets have keyed on Amerindian concepts (rather than words) in a variety of ways. Alurista has utilized the following objects to introduce Amerindian concepts or motifs: plumas, obsidiano, sol, águila, tigre (jaguar), and bronce. (Paradoxically, bronze was unknown to the Aztecs, but then again, Chicano poets use the concept mostly for its color—raza de bronce—rather than its qualities as a material.)

We have given some orientation to the variety of registers within the three major language groups utilized by Alurista: English, Spanish, and Amerindian. Now we need to outline a few of our poet's rich interlinguistic techniques. Once again, Alurista's multilingualism responds to a variety of motives. One of the most common code-switches, as Guadalupe Valdés[33] first recognized, signals a sharp division of domains based on affect and familiarity. In Chicano poetry and fiction the English language is used to represent the Anglo world, and the Spanish language, the Chicano world. Alurista uses this type of bilinguality quite commonly:

> how can anyone misplace barro
>   el barro de la gente . . .
>
>   ("When You Have the Earth in Mouthful")

> perhaps one day, in the angry thrust of my dreams,
> i will discover la verdad en la mentira que me
> rodea . . .
>   . . .
> death in ambush eats tortillas
> chilaquiles con queso
>   y vino de maguey con tunas

> our prayers to be electric
>   to be plugged and light lunas
> ante los santos soles
>   los de rifle y cananas, los de hueso
>   ("Construyendo una balsa")

A type of code-switching which is similar to the one described above is the Spanish identity marker introduced into an English language sequence. Alurista uses órale, ése, ésa, vato, carnal, chicano, chicana, raza, razamía, and so on to establish rapport with his Chicano readers.

> write to your carnales
>   let them know la pachanga's on
>   ("Carnales el amor nos pertenece")

> "i like to have heavy
>   dreams of sarape colors, bato"
>   ("I Like to Sleep")

> we can work it out raza
>   ("We Can Work It Out Raza")

> come down my cheek raza roja
>   ("Come Down My Cheek Raza Roja")

Thus far we have cited fairly straightforward examples of Alurista's code-switching. A more sophisticated variety, a fascinating one in itself, is in his bilingual wordplay. We must not lose sight of the fact that, even as Alurista is one of our most solemn and political poets, he is a master of humor and bilingual sleight of hand. Many of his poems are subtly amusing, others involve a raucous parody, and still others make use of bilingual quips, double entendres, and various figures of speech for thematic purposes. Consider the following lines from "Eternal tripas" (*Nationchild*),

> gather your stones carnales
>   get your canicas back

The use of canicas in the English verse turns the commonplace notion of taking back one's marbles into a fresh and striking bilingual quip. In "Eran, he ran" (*Dawn's Eye*), the lines

       eran, he ran
irán i los días cesar
    del cuento, te cuento chávez
los helicópteros threading
    sombríos hilos
la venta de armas candled
    pendiente
    con jazz, sin monk

string together a sequence of code-switches with striking effects, both stylistic and thematic. The first thirteen poems of *Spik in Glyph?* have the following titles: juan, tu, tree, for, fi, seex, se ven, e it, na in, ten, ee le ven?, tú él, tracy. The titles of the poems, which reify their corresponding numbers 1-13, are played for laughs and also for much more, thematically. Poem number "for" contains the following bilingual pun, working on the double meaning of pedo (fart, but also hassles, trouble, bullshit, etc., in Chicano Spanish), which is combined bilingually with "bean [been] devils":

they bean
devils
exorcizing
puro pedo

The first part of the poem "I Have Found My Flesh" is primarily a parody of highfalutin language both in English and Spanish. Indeed, the point of the poem is amusingly foregrounded by the juxtaposition of empty oratory in Spanish and English.

       where is the oasis where one heavy lays his mind
    to the frescura del arroyo tierno placidly flowing,
    . . .
       i do not know why or stand under that which already
    is, por lo menos en la imaginación de algunas gentes,
    and consequently find myself at the commencement of
    something to be that has terminated su asociación con
    aquello que alguna vez fue. having such been the finished
    product chiseled by the artistry of my will habiendo
    deseado voluntariosamente vagar en el laberinto del libre
    albedrío encuéntrome viviendo.

Revolutions

We have come one full revolution. Having begun with a philol-

GARY D. KELLER

ogy of titles and closed the circle with a philology of -lects, languages, registers, and rhetorics, I have attempted to show how
the anthropological themes—the recuperation of lo chicano, particularly lo amerindio, Aztlán—has in turn affected the Aluristian
poetics of ritual, religion, musicality, performance, and the like,
and given impulse to the switched-on use of language which must
give due consideration to the main players in the formation of the
Chicano identity: indio, español, mestizo, mexicano, anglo, and
other minority or Third World peoples. Having come one full revolution, let us then return to our poet, Alurista,

> once extensions lost
> in the chaos without
> within joyous lakes
> outwitted owls
> of nightly clouds
> howl unbending revolution
> ("Return")

EASTERN MICHIGAN UNIVERSITY

Notes

[1]Juan D. Bruce-Novoa, *Chicano Authors: Inquiry by Interview* (Austin, TX:
University of Texas Press, 1980), p. 276.
[2]Luis Leal, "In Search of Aztlán," *Denver Quarterly*, 16, 3 (Fall 1981), p. 20.
[3]Bruce-Novoa, op. cit., p. 272.
[4]Ibid., p. 274.
[5]Ibid., p. 275.
[6]Ibid., p. 277.
[7]Ibid., pp. 277-78.
[8]Tomás Ybarra-Frausto, "Alurista's Poetics: The Oral, The Bilingual, The
Pre-Columbian," in *Modern Chicano Writers*, ed. Joseph Sommers and Tomás
Ybarra-Frausto (Englewood Cliffs, NJ: Prentice-Hall, 1979), p. 130.
[9]Juan Rodríguez, "La búsqueda de identidad y sus motivos en la literatura
chicana," in *The Identification and Analysis of Chicano Literature*, ed. Francisco
Jiménez (New York: Bilingual Press, 1979), p. 173.
[10]For a good review of this dispute that not only surveys the observations of
Luis Valdez, Augusto Boal, Enrique Buenaventura, Raúl Ruiz, the Teatro Ambu-
lante of Puebla, and others, but also puts them into perspective, see Yvonne
Yarbro-Bejarano, "From *Acto* to *Mito*: A Critical Appraisal of the Teatro Campe-

sino," in *Modern Chicano Writers*, ed. Joseph Sommers and Tomás Ybarra-Frausto (Englewood Cliffs, NJ: Prentice-Hall, 1979), pp. 176-85.

[11]Rodríguez, op. cit., pp. 173-74.

[12]Bruce-Novoa, op. cit., p. 276.

[13]Octavio Romano, "The Historical and Intellectual Presence of Mexican Americans," *El Grito*, 2, 2 (Winter 1969).

[14]Ybarra-Frausto, op. cit., pp. 117-18.

[15]In fairness to Ybarra-Frausto it should be said that in the same article he mitigates his assertion. For example, he does observe that "Alurista's poetry is dense with figurative language through which he recreates a Nahua world view interpreting a metaphorical universe" (p. 120).

[16]*Yo Soy Joaquín* is a more accessible poem than most of Alurista's, yet even here the Bantam pocketbook edition included a section entitled "People and Events in Mexican and Mexican American History," numerous illustrations elucidating the poem, and four pages of material explaining the illustrations in order to provide an orienting apparatus for the reader.

[17]Ybarra-Frausto, op. cit., p. 125.

[18]Ibid., p. 119.

[19]Kukulkán is the Maya name for the same god represented by Quetzalcóatl in the Aztec religion.

[20]Frederick Peterson, *Ancient Mexico* (New York: Capricorn Books, 1962), p. 211.

[21]Ibid., pp. 211-12.

[22]Alurista, "La estética indígena a través del Floricanto de Nezahualcoyotl," *Revista Chicano-Riqueña*, 5, 2 (Spring 1977), p. 56.

[23]Ybarra-Frausto, op. cit., p. 127.

[24]Ibid., p. 128.

[25]Ibid., p. 125.

[26]Bruce-Novoa, op. cit., p. 271.

[27]Gary D. Keller, "The Literary Strategems Available to the Bilingual Chicano Writer," in *The Identification and Analysis of Chicano Literature*, ed. Francisco Jiménez (New York: Bilingual Press, 1979), p. 290.

[28]Bruce-Novoa, op. cit., pp. 271-72.

[29]Ibid., p. 272.

[30]Gary D. Keller, op. cit., pp. 263-316.

[31]Gary D. Keller, "Toward a Stylistic Analysis of Bilingual Texts: From Ernest Hemingway to Contemporary Boricua and Chicano Literature," in *The Analysis of Hispanic Texts: Current Trends in Methodology*, eds. Mary A. Beck, Lisa E. Davis, José Hernández, Gary D. Keller, and Isabel C. Tarán (New York: Bilingual Press, 1976), pp. 130-49.

[32]Egla Morales Blouin, "Símbolos y motivos nahuas en la literatura chicana," in *The Identification and Analysis of Chicano Literature*, ed. Francisco Jiménez (New York: Bilingual Press, 1979), pp. 179-90.

[33]See Guadalupe Valdés-Fallis, "The Sociolinguistics of Chicano Literature: Towards an Analysis of the Role and Function of Language Alternation in Contemporary Bilingual Poetry," *Point of Contact/Punto de contacto*, 1, 4 (1977), pp. 30-39, and Guadalupe Valdés-Fallis, "Code-Switching in Bilingual Chicano Poetry," *Hispania*, 59 (1976), pp. 877-86.

pa'

— *mis hijos tizoc, maoxiim, zamna y zahi*

— *mi compañera xelina*

— *mis primeros editores, octavio romano
y herminio ríos*

— *mis primeros críticos, gus segade
y juan gómez-quiñones*

— *el pueblo en pie de lucha dondequiera
que ésta se manifieste*

nationchild plumaroja

1969–1972

"Once a man has vanquished fear, he is free from it for the rest of his life because, instead of fear, he has acquired clarity—a clarity of mind which erases fear. By then a man knows his desires, he knows how to satisfy those desires. He can anticipate the new steps of learning, and a sharp clarity surrounds everything. The man feels that nothing is concealed. . . . It gives him the assurance he can do anything he pleases, for he sees clearly into everything. And he is courageous because he is clear and he stops at nothing because he is clear. But all that is a mistake; it is like something incomplete. If the man yields to this make believe power, he has succumbed to his second enemy and will fumble with learning. He will rush when he should be patient, or he will be patient when he should rush."

Don Juan, from *The Teachings*

 *nopal*

WE WOULD HAVE BEEN
RELIEVED WITH DEATH

we would have been relieved with death
    i know
en el sillón espero el pelo blanco
        de seda rapping
        to me lips labios rojos
en guitarra corrida de arena en llamas
       if burnt; carne quemada (chicharrón)
relief
    tal vez cansado de esperar
        sin sueño
i will dream again
        satisfecho, relajado en mi papel
para encontrarlo
gratis and live
even if relieved,
        i would have been
sin carrera, sin apresurarme
           a la muerte
no iré a mi entierro
    my epitaph will be blank in my solace

SALSA CON CRACKERS

salsa con crackers
¿cómo? con la boca
prelogical fruit
    prehistorical experience entre las palmas
entrando a preprimaria
y a la salida
    after school con chona
a las quesadillas
    de la bruja con limones embotellados

3

and cucumbers con chile piquín
—a veces jícama
a veces nada—sin dinero without friends
pobre and abandoned; hungry
crackers do not quench my pangs
    my gut
swelled
tengo hambre
        crackers do not show their fangs
no bite, no poison or enchantment
sin sabor o nutrimiento
even con salsa
        arid, dry, desiertas de calor

I HAVE FOUND MY FLESH

where is the oasis where one heavy lays his mind
to the frescura del arroyo tierno placidly flowing,
such a rose bud would sprouting en el centro del
desierto sin circunferencia more often than not i've
interrogated myself? to discover, compounded with a
multitude of textured answers, sin encontrar respuesta
alguna he decidido no preguntar, dejar mi pasión por
el entendimiento y descubrir que ante the vacuum which
the lack of action originates caos nace en el orden,
la secuencia.
    i do not know why or stand under that which already
is, por lo menos en la imaginación de algunas gentes,
and consequently find myself at the commencement of
something to be that has terminated su asociación con
aquello que alguna vez fue. having such been the finished
product chiseled by the artistry of my will habiendo
deseado voluntariosamente vagar en el laberinto del libre
albedrío encuéntrome viviendo.
    henceforth i can only do but that which the assertion
of my self implies in the form of a must. little less
puede resultar ante al encuentro accidental con la muerte
forging the skeleton of its structure into a mobile
having conquered time in its cooperation with fixating

space i can only cry or die; however i, being one never
to mind my mind, have chosen the exception to my
minding it. i suffer y estoy vivo en el acto de mi afecto
por la muerte.

> tan cerca como el sol
>> la muerte acecha y brilla en mi balcón
> triste ilusión eterna la que me fija
> anchored to my toil
>>> me muevo con las olas
>> azoto las rocas con mi pecho

standing under moonful of bones
i could die naked
derretido sobre cobble stones
a media calle
ante su semblante rostro emaciado
> i have found my flesh alive
en el recuerdo pestilente de su presencia
i live, i love
i cry in the desert aliviado

CONSTRUYENDO UNA BALSA

perhaps one day, in the angry thrust of my dreams,
i will discover la verdad en la mentira que me
rodea. at the pinnacle of my climb clouds episode
in sequence to that which once was, i will eat mis
tacos con salsa without fearing a colibrí to come
and such mi miel i will go to misa, to the church
where to the saints we light velas. and we know nothing
nor do i see any more stars than those assigned to me
by light years and space bondage.

in view of such arid limitations pretendo convertir
mis sueños en los que me encuentro ante el aroma que
mi piel despide evaporating now, to rain mole tomorrow.
it is then no surprise or misguided expectation that
materializes itself in the form of calavera romántica
que cena con la muerte, tortilla en mano and entirely
committed to the act of being. what, as an obstacle, goal
or inclination to discover of seems quite irrelevant in

view of the how, within which my behavior is implicit.
el estilo y la manera en que mi forma se desenvuelve
undergoing metamorphosis in amphibious terrains es,
entonces, el medio primordial
en que el palpitar de mis venas sufre ante la danza
y los manjares de chilimaíz que brotan de la
mesa and for my hunger.
    de tal manera que mi ira resultará inevitablemente
como la tarde que llora ante la presencia de la luna
y de la noche que se avecina. no more to bear
the burden on the shoulders put my mind away
para que nadie meta el codo en aquel mole.
    o en salsa de cera
    en comida veladoras nunca
la cocina de barro y de frijoles pintos
manchados en la herida, melting
construyendo una balsa
(la travesía es difícil)
death in ambush eats tortillas
chilaquiles con queso
    y vino de maguey con tunas
our prayers to be electric
        to be plugged and light lunas
ante los santos soles
    los de rifle y cananas, los de hueso

SPITTING THE WOUNDS OFF MY FIRE

spitting the wounds off my fire
    i cried
grité en el ocaso de la tarde
    cuya capa de nubes me cubre y arde
"among the nations
    as it is among individuals
respect for the rights of others
      is peace"
benito juárez came to mind
bienestar social le llaman
    limosnas que ciegan

en mi mano de polvo y lodo nunca
la dignidad terciopelo verde
    suave y acariciante
        ante el roce de mi piel
dignity in my being chicano
    demands respect
en mi fe yace mi error
    mi fe en el conocimiento terso
i failed to understand the lack of
    in him from whom
i once demanded (dignity unknown)

CHICANO COMMENCEMENT

chicano commencement
    exercising freedom, breathing
    in zapata's gown
        i found myself graduating
me encontré en el comienzo
    en el origen-principio
de mi raza-creciente
    en lágrimas ante el techo de mi choza
tata chente, gonzález, pancho cervantes
reunidos
    furia en pecho pancho saiz
issy chávez, irma castro
    todos juntos en el rezo
a nuestra raza la misa
a beginning seed of end to sorrow
    self pity and quiet never; when
the boil is on
    up tight today
    loose winds, caress mountains
tequila y salsa con tortillas
    de maíz
  nace apenas in our tassel

PIEDRA ROCA NIEBLA

piedra roca niebla
heavy lid of waterfalls on burnt cheeks
ojos rojos de coraje en plumas de quetzal
fixated mound of moonful
    of dreams frustrated leaps
    dripping faucet bleeding thirst
i in the pond sink never
ranas desiertas en flores de pantano
derramando sinfonías en el velo luna noche
piedra roca
    niebla piedra roca
    piedra niebla
    roca piedra (pesada azucena de dolor)
tengo sed
mejillas misteriosas medusas
caballeros tigres montañas de voluntad
chanting in the dusk cavern of sensuous pebbles
stones
    precious tears aged in sulphur
rock
    rhythmic arrows bathed in war paint
fog festival of rising red struggle (sink never)

BARRIENDO LAS HOJAS SECAS

barriendo las hojas secas
    rastrillo en mano de pizca
la casa en ruinas de sueños de baranda
climbing fences ivy covered huts (dogs barking)
wire walls transparent dividers
    away, away — lejos de mis brazos
mi mano no alcanza y mi escoba no barre
    no barre el polvo
        las hojas
    el dolor y la pobreza lloran rocas
lavando las ventanas de cartón en el verano
sulphur afternoons wind glooms — hair flows dark

8

negros ojos
        negra suerte en el jardín de yerbas
weeds in solitude thrusting isolation saturdays
        wooden webs for fences fragile (spiders in the grass)
mowed lawn of dusty cans cardboard and nails
"buenas tardes"
        buenas!?
        buenas pa' qué!
            pa' nada!
pa' barrer, pa' respirar, pa' soñar (en hojas secas)

RIDE BICYCLE PAPERBOY

ride bicycle paperboy
        juanita on handle bars hanging
clinging to raspado dreams
ride, ride
        kitchen hungry child
tortillas y frijoles velas de esperanza
feed juanita — sell the papers, ride
naciste pa' pedalear
        jorge neverstare
neverstare at the sunrise of your doom
doom you may find in outhouse
paint the planks
        ride in the absent laceration gone
to madera vieja
        splintered afternoon set fire
if only the ice of your raspado
        turn your dreams to miel
feed juanita
        ride your bike
sell your paper
        burn your outhouse
paint the walls and have an ice cone
never jorge child stare
at the sunrise of your doom (pull the shades
                find the sunset on the water
                melting to begin)

to build a bicycle
        to ride
    your own
to swim
    raspado sweat on chest
con valor (el tuyo)
        vigila las calles — ride
y el bienestar de tu raza
        de la especie
(la humana) opuesta sólo a la muerte
dedicada a tierra fértil
    no para explotar
only to reap fruit
        earth's tribute to humankind (ness)
maybe
        vigila, guarda tu suerte
guarda el destino en tus manos
    ride

DEATH RIDING ON A SODA CRACKER

death riding on a soda cracker
    hassling badges and clubs at hand
            to crack skulls
    to crack walls
        to crack death on adobe halls
    man, don't know the hassle of his badge
                    the clubbing kill
            or he don't know what's living
he don't know, no sabe nada
                    absolutamente nada
vacío su pecho de emociones rosas rojas
        verdes realidades
no sabe nada
    the man, he cannot see carnales
carnales de pedernal
    en la paja de este mundo
            una chispa prende el fuego
light up chicano bato

enciéndase sola carnala y encienda
encienda la paja
on the comal get our tortillas going
feed our children con frijoles
con la sangre of our fuego
a los niños, nuestros hijos alimenta
tráeles to our mundo nuevo
al mundo de raza fuego
donde chicanos descubren realidades
en verdades de ternura
la revolución desnuda
in the open thrust of platitudes
of reactionary attitudes
of apathy, avergonzada
riding on a soda cracker
blindness in helmeted skull
sucia muerte negro y blanco, colorblind
colorculture blind
se ha olvidado de su vida
to remember goldcoingod
le ha prendido veladoras a su dios
dios, moneda; oro y plata pisoteante

WHEN YOU HAVE THE EARTH IN MOUTHFUL

when you have the earth in mouthful
to chew con los dientes de esperanza
un sueño de pueblos rojos
how can anyone misplace barro
el barro de la gente en notas
(musicales) tardes de espera
y espera, y espera
sin que el sol se acueste, no
aparece el dolor lunar en carnes
y el barro no se cuece
como un sueño en la mano
chicanos do not lose sueños
y de sí son propios dueños

chicanos, mechicano dreams
y los sueños que acosan durante la comida
are the same dreams that fácilmente
find the opening cavern to the labyrinth of
chains. chains are fallen. decrepit find
the bunk in cell. slept on the beach
for a while. lights on, guards pacing
cannot find the recovery of
sleep. and cannot wait for the crepuscle.
cannot lose the dream for chicanos shall
lose ourselves. and of ourselves we are
masters. chicano masters of chicano
sueños de color frijoles con salsa y con
cebolla. dentro de la campana que
repica hidalgo — fuera de la iglesia
el padre clama justicia, libertad y
tierra. dentro de ella nunca existió
dicho sueño — no pa'l pueblo, no pa' la
raza, pa' la gente; pa' nosotros
nada. "ni ma' carnal" me dice
el bato; "se acabó la onda." i don't
understand that kind of payasadas.
con mi gente no se juega. a mis
niños no les quita nadie los frijoles.
se acabó la espera mr. jones,
"señor" jones (perdone usté "patrón").
i don't care if you call yourself my uncle
and remind me that you ain't my
dad. my dad? mi padre era
zapata, juárez y madero mis
hermanos corky el león, chávez
el palomo, y los berets they are my
brothers. mis carnales son chicanos.
mis carnales son humanos mr. jones.
and the relativity of your coin
makes you meaningless. to me to all
who call themselves i, and assert
su sangre y su valor de cuero, de
hueso colorado. you are meaningless
mr. jones. and tell your vieja mrs.
robinson — your ex-wife frigid man!

that we ain't falling for sus faldas ni
cortejos. our barro digs on warmth and
you mr. jones are a frigidair of pestilence.
    an ice joke on your martini
    cubical skull you got
    we weep and in lakes round flow
    y our raza se baña en arroyos
    donde cantan las ranas con guitarras
    y los grillos hacen el falsete
    we got our razared
        we got our barro
    we don't need your "holy" breath

CARNALES EL AMOR
NOS PERTENECE

carnales el amor nos pertenece
    raza bronce no perece
    en este clima no muere
nos pertenecen las calles, el barrio
    the phone posts and electric bulbs
the mailboxes are ours to use
    in the afternoon a letter send
to other chicanos, with blood seal it
    settle the foggy paper into flight
        free the spacious lines
        empty of figures, write
write to your carnales
    let them know la pachanga's on
on today for all
        pa' todos to feel alright
pa' los que queran frijoles
    pa' los que queran cañones
there will be a flying bird in the sky
        to sit down and cry by
y pa' los que queran liberta'
        there will be tequila raza
con sal y limón

EVENFLO BOTTLE FEED

evenflo bottle feed
    to any child
water boiled drink
    no milk give
rocking in the cradle
    of his birth
pa' soñar bonito
      pos aquí ajuera
'ta muy feo
metido en la botella el barco
    without breeze of water
        sail to sea, to shore
a la orilla del río
        donde el bosque se espesa
soup of sulphur and oxide hopes
there in the bottle
    el cerdo de la bureaucracy
devora the entrails of his skull
    inside out color
a shadow surplusultranill
dispensable sombra de botella
    comercial mamadera cristal

CUANDO LA CUCARACHA CAMINE

cuando la cucaracha camine
    en our libertad crucificada
on the wooden planks petrified statues
on the nail a cross beneath a man
we will know the sound
    the bells of our impatience gone, by
waterfallen sounds of solitude to joy
i was then a little altar boy, kneeling
while the cucaracha crawled
muddling through the crumbs the cucaracha
crawled, and crawled; dragging her soul
not knowing bread to be abundant she lacked

14

and went hungry
        pangs and clamor
to be heard in the dusk of a
        morning dew
        chicano mass
to preach about the kingdom of man and woman
(god has been ruler long enough as god)
men and women have to learn themselves about
one another, to love each other
(chicanos will then preach of the kingdom of god)

BY THE GENTLE FLAPPING
OF A PALM, ON THE STEPS

by the gentle flapping of a palm, on the steps
        outside sitting, i find a lot of injustice inside
my arms wrapped around in the winter
neck up turned (built-in scarf)
        my bones freeze before the frigid pig
lacking of warm blood turned bluebadge man
        of white to serve,
                the retrograde status quo
        not the people, white workers, disillusioned youth
        black souls
                not chicano hearts, or red or yellow
        skins, not the east not buddha
                (the lover of mankind)
        not any warm blooded mammalian
                the pig a hog leg in his holster
frigid armature, poor imitation of homo sapiens
and the breeze shatters my eye lids
        half closed in desperation to be blind
ugliness wants us to run away
        let your blood boil, it's been frozen
get inside of yourself carnal
        get your fire

TAZA DE BARRO EN
LA QUE BEBO MI CAFÉ

taza de barro en la que bebo mi café
    humo pendiente de mis labios se evapora
there is time still in the water falls of anger
chicanos en el barrio
        esperanza en cancerosa célula
        en el capitalismo radica la moneda
en el socialismo viven los hombres y las mujeres
        viven como pueblo entre hermanos y hermanas
no como zombies cuerpos
entre robots traga monedas
    carga pistola y mace
          helmeted skulls
    to serve you unto death
in capitalism there is a choice
    we can die poisoned by decrepit,
    anachronic socio-political institutions,
    (we can die slowly)
or we can die quickly
    massacred in our cry for justice

LET YOURSELF BE SIDETRACKED
BY YOUR GÜIRO

let yourself be sidetracked by your güiro
carnal let yourself be free
to do your music when your heart pounds
in the melody of your ringing ears
unto death do not allow your love to pass
unto life embrace other carnales
help each other sweat the day away
eat your tortillas together
carnales we gotta share our joys
in the quetzal pride
on the pyramid of sun glaze birth
get together
make your music

16

make your canto raza
make your barrios
make your lives carnales
make la raza live
unto life juntos
        bajo el sol de nuestros padres

I LIKE TO SLEEP

"i like to sleep
        with a lot of sarapes on me, man"
"i like to have heavy
        dreams of sarape colors, bato"
we hear and fail
        to listen or even understand
we find ourselves in a shell
        of corporation, military nightmares
of success, of co in
                co opt
                cut out
                    sp
                            lit
                        go
                            n
                                e
y el bato likes heavy dreams
        and doesn't turn on to smog
he don't like coinshells
        he knows, la vida
no vale nada sin tierra
        sin libertad

THINKING IS THE BEST WAY

thinking is the best way
          to travel by the clouds
          and sink in flower tones
          in foam fluorescent sands
to travel in free associations
todos juntos, nosotros
ya no va a haber pedo carnal
          ahora clickeamos juntos
la raza is together bato
          it ain't never gonna break
esta raza no se quebra carnal
'cause we gonna think it out
          together, juntos
in one thought la razaroja
          can be told al mundo
a todo el mundo, juntos we will
          discuss, argue
               and disagree
          and find new ondas
ondas on which we can find
          a new nosotros
          a raza nueva

HEAVY DRAG STREET OF SMOG

heavy drag street of smog
shadowed shelter of adobe blocks
i am reminded of
carnala
     la raza es de bronce
de piel sedosas carnes
en las que descubro la cascada de pelo
          que te acaricia
          que te da calor
descubro a margarita
          entre las flores aroma de barrio
          de ternura tarde

18

       tarde, cansado de esperar
i find no time for fighting other chicanos
i can only hate in them
     what i lack in myself, la raza's proud
carnala
     la raza es de bronce
finding my way in the fog
a butterfly
a dream
a choza pa' descansar la cabeza

 *xochitl*

TUNING FLOWER TONES

tuning flower tones
guitarra sings in serenata
the twanging, twanging, tone
   to tablas tuned
the thumping of a rhythm shoe
tapping, tapping, taconeo
y el latido de la sangre
en el corazón explota
las burbujas del sol
el de cuauhtémoc, tizoc
o el plumado moctezuma
el sol de la tierra
the plantation pains
and pangs of hungry lives
trabajando en la cosecha
today, we live in the waste pockets
   of the city wild barrios
batos locos en protesta social
   caminando en clickas
together in the dusk of orgullo
humming hums of slow paced tunes
seeking peace

BECAUSE LA RAZA IS TIRED

because la raza is tired
i find time in molasses thick
we cannot wait
  because la raza is tired
we cannot wait
the moving red sun is out
   to shine a crystal dream
to walk an autumn leaf to earthy drought

to bring water in cubetas
                put out fire of red uniform
arriving to feed on ashes
en las ruinas calaveras rocas
        tristes recuerdos vacíos of a dead people
genocide, genocide
we cannot wait, because
wait because la raza
tired, torn we cannot wait
while la raza's being born

WALKING DOWN

walking down
        abajo, abajo hacia el cristiano
        suelo de licor, de vinos
        de uvas aplastadas gentes
la raza
        walking down church yard road
epitaph written in confessionary box
        ready to be buried
nunca
        las campanas del pueblo
        repicando afuera pa' que el campesino
        pa' que el campesino las oiga
el entierro de la gente
        bajo árida tierra
        seca cosecha, sin maíz
        arroz o frijoles
walking down
        down the christian licorice floor
        de anís y de azucenas
        incienso y bosque
bosque de pinos occidentales

TAL VEZ PORQUE TE QUIERO

tal vez porque te quiero
    raza mía
molten bronze unto a god
    chicano-hermano, hermana chicana
derretido en las llamas
    razasol
because i kneel before you
weeping in my hunger's joy
caring not for nothing cold
    but the people razared
de calor que en borbotones nace
calienta los frijoles, el arroz
        y las tortillas
perhaps that's why i love you
    razared
    rojaraza
  razamía
tal vez porque
    vez porque te quiero
porque te quiero
    te quiero todavía
razamía

THROUGH THE FENCES
THAT SURROUND YOU, GRITA

through the fences that surround you, grita
yell through your heart clamored hope
dreams be crystalized in the struggle of today
a gritar — con el ardor de la sangre
    ¡viva la raza! ¡que viva!
    que viva, pa' siempre
si tu alma llora es porque la muerte
la calavera te acecha, mas lucha, lucha
la muerte en azufre espera
carnal, tu tropiezo añora
mas no, ¡nunca!

carga tu pistola en mano y grita
    ¡viva la raza! ¡que viva!
¡porque la raza es de bronce!
    de barro nuestras facciones
    y de oro son nuestros sones
    canta carnal
    grita y canta por la raza
que la revolución truene
    que nosotros venceremos, venceremos
venceremos

BUILT-IN CHAINS VACATIONS PAID

built-in chains vacations paid
    social security
    and retirement soon to come (in velvet)
barf the opium idiot box zombies eat
machine bolts
    attached and riveted, en la cruz
    agonizantes and apathetic
placing bets
    rooting teams and clamoring
    blood
¡que se vea sangre!
    ¡sangre! sangre de color ... ¡no blanca!
    sangre muerta pulsa en sus alambres
la máquina se envenena
    and stupefied zombi men
sterilized, homogenized
    objective as a victim of its object
    itself the target
    of a broken dream, in yesterday's rain
excreted on the pavement, concrete wall
run over by its own wheels, gears blind
vacations paid (redeemable when dead).

JUAN DIEGO

juan diego
chicano hermano
revolucionaria raza
visión de villa
en la madre
morena frente rojiza
¡nosotros!
todos nosotros
in motion
pendulum swing en el cielo
¡carnal!
carnal, ¿sabes qué?
lo que pasa
es que
    i'm basically happy
aunque mi general villa
quera llevarse al amor
la mecedora
la mujer del movimiento
la soldadera colorada

BORN IN THE STEPS
OF A DESERT

born in the steps of a desert
on the sand a lagartija
lizard thirst that of our raza
acostumbrados al hambre
nos damos cuenta en la sangre
en la muerte
    rojas tardes esperanzas
de dolor y de agonía
la raza sufre y conoce
    la raza knows much of back pain
    of working, sweating and dying
así, así raza
comprendamos el desierto

y con agua
quench our sueños
quench the throats that thirst for water
drink to live today, mañana
mañana y ayer are instants
today, ahorita
la lluvia
la de truenos
la de gotas y relámpagos
riega mi jardín entero

ME RETIRO CON MIS SUEÑOS

me retiro con mis sueños
con las plumas de guerrero
con el hacha de tizoc
        el artista, el hechicero
plumas ... feathers on the forehead
clay ... barro en los dedos
anointed raza de fuego
burning and yelling and living
to die someday in the struggle
la revolución, la raza
gente, gente roja
con historia
con presente corazón en mano
gente, people, raza
        willing and in fire consuming
entre mis sueños y el fuego
        poco es el frío de mis huesos
sun glazed in our sweat
        the struggle
la revolución, la raza
la de palmas de guerrero rojo fuego

MI MIND

mi mind
    constipated with tortillas
    is found to be with joy, con alegría
    y con salsa colorada piel
    de bronce
    sedabrown
a people glazed in barro
flying to the pyramids where the sun strolls
casting shadows of sorrowful wounds
lacerations casted racist fever
el menjurge de mago
    —hechicero chicano
    —frijol grabado en la frente
heals, alivia cold calenturas
con sangre pulsante
    —hirviendo en la muchedumbre
la raza
a people born in the struggle
la lucha
la luna llena
    —las tortillas de mi sol
la libertad, la nuestra

TUS DEDOS
LA TIERRA CUBRE

tus dedos la tierra cubre
la raza vive en la tierra
sembrada la tierra es nuestra
labrada, llorada (en sangre sudada)
frente en alto vibra bronce
venerando al sol moreno
—calor que corre en las venas
valor que vive en los hechos
en la choza de la gente
encuentro en comal frijoles
las tortillas sudan fuego

27

y la salsa llora sangre
encuentro la raza nueva
la que con la mar se acoge
la que con la tierra duerme
en las raíces almohadas
en las palmeras los sueños
en los sueños brotan llamas
en la vida arde la carne
  suda la revolución
  la raza late, y se impone
  y la sangre es derramada

COME DOWN MY CHEEK RAZA ROJA

come down my cheek raza roja
to caress mis pómulos salientes
  —i want to kiss the mejilla that adorns
  bronce brocado
tu boca exhaling el espíritu de la sangre
nuestra sangre
  boiling in the backyard
thrust into the open callejones
cactus field of rocks and polvo
  y tierra húmeda
in our macetas
a semilla
  a possible nacimiento
¡raza!
¡¡raza!!
  take the time to be born
take time by the neck
  turn it into an arado
  cultivate el maíz de nuestra
identidad indígena
  a la vida, a la muerte
al nacimiento de un nopal

COCO, COCO

coco, coco basin headed programed man
      pistoled mouthed
      shotgun carrier to protect
hassle, hassle plated badge recorded tape
      que te lleva, que te agarra
      que te come; ya me dice la mamá
"se llevaron al padre
      al hermano
      y al tata le colgaron de su orgullo en un papel"
coco, coco
    vienes coco, sin caballo
    sin estribos y sin silla
coco, coco
    vienes coco ya montado
      ya pegado a tus botones
      con tus máquinas de hiel
coco eras tú, coco, coco
    de orgánica manera
      ya el miedo, ya la sed
      pero ahora; we don't know you
mounted, riding on conveyor belt
inorganic ... coco, coco basin headed death
                and frigid breath

I HAD CHILAQUILES

i had chilaquiles
    salsa joy and onion fire to pretend
      deafness to tambores   thirsting
                        gasping
                        begging
i had chilaquiles
      to share in ollas de color — pintadas jarras
      white man dug our spice and shun our breath
      he came to us to eat
          and ran

and ran in his forgetfulness
of us, of our salsa de colores (yace dios)
    en el pan de los abuelos
    in the clamor of their toil
        sembrando maíz
    slapping tortillas on their palms
a shape is born
    to tear and mingle in tomates
to burn and weep in chile verde
        o colorado
to be the universe of our hunger's vision
i heard tortillas boil, and maíz was broken

BEFORE THE FLESH IN BONES

before the flesh in bones
    took shape and dialogued
        in the breakfast of tortillas
    blind to los cielos y la tierra,
    we were a wooden image,
a projection of the dioses que le hablaban
molcajetes volaron en protesta
        atrapados entre una opresión enjuta de madera
    y un destino de cadenas y promesas
    de salsas que elaboran sentimientos
        (lacking then in us)
la sangre carecía de albergue
    and the rivers of blood no circulaban
¿por qué? ¿por qué ... ? ¿qué tenía que pasar? ¿quién
                    habría de morir?
    porque no hablaba con los dioses
este cuerpo de madera
        había de ser quemado.
they who crawl and fly al fuego se lanzaron
la serpiente emplumada se hizo sol y el cascabel ...
    el cascabel en víbora prendido
comenzó la música que hizo al pueblo de fuego.

NUESTRA CASA — DENVER '69

cuetes de malinches lenguas
     preoccupied statues
     piedras entumidas, sin calor
        y sin amor moreno
el carnalismo nace como la tuna
     entre espinas de dulzura
     el color sarape de contrastes
y la marcha
     la marcha-mestiza
     sentimientos que flotan en el aire — la bandera
razaroja praying to the sun marchando en la misa
     power to las manos que trabajan
     power to all who dig tortillas
y que se bañan en sudor salado
     trabajando en penitencia
        haciendo liberación
piernas waking to the marcha of our pueblo
our gente, en los barrios
     en las escuelas
     en las canerías
     en la pizca
     en la calle (our steps are measured)
¡chale! we can't take no measurement ... ¡chale!
no more rezos de rodillas
no more apologies por ser de carne
     y de hueso
porque tenemos hambre and our children
     are singing con orgullo
the children are just beginning to be people
  los pueblos ya espinados are hungry
    hungry for tunas
     for dulzura
     por amor de carnales
nuestra casa es nuestra casa
     tenemos que laborar juntos
     tenemos que organizar the disarray left
  by he, the master of cadenas of oppression
     tenemos que construir de adobecorazón
     a casacalor de fuego libertad

nuestra raza es nuestra raza
   and the tunas of our struggle
are eaten en nuestra casa.
   fuera muebles coloniales
   we gonna sleep with sarapes
to dream our sueños de fuego
to wake el espíritu que vibra
   en la sangre que nuestra razaroja
          ya llora,
          ya clama justicia
de dos caras we've been born
nuestra madre, mujer india-asiática
nuestro padre el europeo-africano
    nuestro corazón mestizo
   has now grown bigotes, brochas y hasta pelos
con el frijol en la frente,
with cheekbones facing el sol encuerado
    drilling freedom in the clouds
la bandera mexicana kissed the heights
     kissed corazones
   y entre gritos el espíritu moreno
thrusting flechas in the statues
    tongues once forked are silent
   quiet ante la verdad morena
that our suns have calentado
casa raza, razaraza, carnalrojo
ríe, canta risk your life for la causa
    live for la revolución que nace ya en nuestra
                 casa

A CHILD TO BE BORN

a child to be born
    `pregnant is the continente
el barro y la raza
    to bear aztlán on our forehead
el niño como pájaro
    en su vuelo de colores cantos
       guió a tenoch hacia el águila

32

el niño dentro del vientre semilla
        una madretierraroja le acaricia
aztlán, aztlán of the continent that bears child
        tu madre es — el continentetierraroja
where the crickets call the birth
        and the ranas arrullan al nacido
y las víboras del mar siguen a la campanita
        por donde pueden pasar los de adelante
and the ones in the back se quedarán
                aztlán, aztlán
the semilla que plantó nuestro padre quetzalcoatl
        ya germina
        en el vientre de nuestra
                madrecontinentetierra, amerindia
nationchild de su padrecarnalismo kukulcán

BLOW UP TIGHT TO FLY

blow up tight to fly
        in the nubes of our joy
raza never die
        mujer eterna raza
raza nueva, raza raza
in the sarapes find the truth
en los colores contrastes de tu piel
razaroja, razablack,
                up tight
today, in the swamps of pestilence
heavy dreams on our shoulders
an open redpath to follow
libres, al fin
razalibre
razanace
razaroja
fly in up-tight blow

LOS TAMBORES,
LOS TAMBORES

los tambores, los tambores
tocan, tocan
en la puerta raza
tocan, tocan
open the wounds of your heart
to the sun, to the sun
burn, burn raza
mientras los tambores
tocan, tocan
corazón ama
llora y vive
corazón

LA CALABAZA IS GONNA

la calabaza is gonna
            turn into a car
to drive in midnight abrelatas
for all types of latas
an opening opportunity dark
in the dusk of a pumpkin
such are dreams
sueños pesados de esperanza
la realidad de frijoles hierve,
el adobe ya aparece
to wake
in crimson dawns
and wet sidewalks
and fog
and stench
dark dusk slipper
lost in a half night

 *serpiente*

WE CAN WORK IT OUT
RAZA

we can work it out raza
our troubles mutual
over a plate of frijoles
we'll have our tortillas be warmed
and live together
la raza junta
chicanos free from cold cubicles
la raza nueva
while the owl meditates cactus dreams
la raza marches on with machetes
a la selva pizca siembra
pa' construir la nueva raza tradición
to smoke peace out of a love pipe pasto
sheep grazing on cheeks, while
sitting en la junta raza nueva
trouble conflict chingaderas
we can work
   can work
      work them out
to remain juntos

DOWN WALLED ALLEYS MARKED

down walled alleys marked
   "el grifo de la logan"
   con la tradición del "quí quí rí quí"
el gallo anciano sabio
el patriarca de la logan
de los callejones
entre los garages
detrás de la tortillería
bajo el poste

con la raza meets
in the birth of a night
discovering the flicker of dawn
sun of pyramids
sun of suns to grow red
fire beams and warmth
kicking a can full of butts, split
walk
      down marked
      walled alleys
callejones de cartón y lata

OUT THE ALLEY OUR SOUL AWAITS US

out the alley our soul awaits us
to meet on pebbled streets the breeze
the bongo rhythm of our thumping heart
to catch the wind the odor and the flesh
to launch our gaze on once lost hopes
a candle
sitting in lonely stare
a tear
irrigating our cheekbone high lands
pyramids, feathers and rituals of love
people in the dusk afternoon of a cloudy horizon
love
quetzalcoatl in life rejoices
and we walk down age carved alleys
running to find alma, sangre y aliento
feathers in stomach gnaw melancholiac ulcers
and huitzilopochtli drinks our blood
raza rain in tlaloc's agony
raza run to the sun and sing
of the barrio
and the soft winds that flagellate our skeleton

TAL VEZ EN EL AMANECER

tal vez en el amanecer
la nieve de tu sangre en agua se convierte
fría realidad, fea sombra
disappear
your welcome is over, genocide
go hunt yourself in suicide
people eat tortillas
while the rooster of the cannery
the whistle blows, the silence of a
morning breaks
and the máquina camina
con el sudor de la raza
el aceite en las aceras
leaves fallen during a lost season
another year
another page to fill, a can of beer
such is the want of a máquina
a chicano takes a siesta only in
    the meditation of our struggle
    in the consecration of our people red
    raza
    tal vez en el amanecer

LAS CANANAS Y EL CALVARIO

las cananas y el calvario
dos hermanos en su muerte
    bullets seven shot and planted
        tear, tear bullet
que yo te veo en mi machete
        ignored you will find yourself
        calvario, penitencia
te desea mi flagelado cuerpo
        parado en el corazón
        rock of solitude
            now
      burning

our penitence de rodillas
          nunca encontrará la muerte
el carnaval de dolor y las máscaras de cristo
     brutalized facades in hiding
all masks be fallen, be flown
          al rugido de una flecha
las cananas en el barrio
               la liberación calvario
"mejor muerto y bien parado
than beg living de rodillas"

LABYRINTH OF SCARRED HEARTS

labyrinth of scarred hearts
     wounded in the sown struggle
     sproutings in the making of a
          historical leaf of radical movement
a people powered in red clad faith
en penitencia guerrera
en revolución morena grasp
     serene hands on the earth
plowing, plowing
     watering in tears for torn backs
and burning perspiration in the fields
a few paths lead, follow and walk
          alone, to the light out the cueva
out the solitude caverna de miedo
on
to the path that has a heart
a nomad drinking agua de barro
cortando la maleza
     con machete voluntad, cutting the earth
healing the wounds planting barro
          planting paths with heart
               and clarity

CLAMPED ALMAS

clamping las almas de un pueblo
        de nuestra gente que vibra
         cuya cola cascabel, cascabelea
                rattle, rattlecoil
let the clamored hope to breathe, ...
                breathe!
en el pecho de aztlán
          —el soplo de dios quetzal
          —culebra tierra de barro
tear the brazos off the máquina
        off with its mediatized head
let the tuercas gorge and splatter
for el corazón is mourning
where spades are called machetes
      donde las armas son cuetes
          ruido verdad y guitarras
let the last alambre burn and breath be rattled

CRIOLLO YOU LIVED PROHIBITION

criollo you lived prohibition
        tras la cerca del ibero
la colonia tu tortilla
        tu techo, the mestizo's agonía
     tus jardines el sudor de aquel vendido
     and your plantations of thievery
     encueradas al sol testimony
        con espigas y maíz
la cosecha de un pueblo robaste
     y robas vestido aun ahora
     y violas la manta y te llamas chicano
     y chupas la sangre del barrio
     y te dicen batman — yankee sacón!
face your color, face your face
and then mírame a los ojos
parejo si te atreves
a sudar conmigo en las tareas de la tierra

CORAZÓN LÁPIDA

on the history of our wounds
the epitaph of our hearts pounds
        to a cuerpo de carne
roja sangre tocapuertas, toca
        el alma
el espíritu que cascabeleando vuela
vibramuerte a través de un evil-eye
        o una aguja marker en la carne
        of a tierra arrebatada
where the lápida of our flesh
        shall caress the stolen land
    and kiss the rocas, a mother
indiamuerte en plumas
        y en cananas
junto a la tumba, la madre!
        our sangre, la resurrección morena

LENGUAGARGANTA ACALLECIDA

lenguagarganta acallecida en seco ardor,
in the fire picazón that boils a breath.
la carne de los labios brama.
        the palabras that mutiny a tongue
            crave to be spilt en llamas
            to splatter paredes arrugadas
            upon which silence falls;
        and the rooftops of tongues
            crawl in flight to the cuevas
            in prayers de rodillas laceradas
            pesadillas y recuerdos fried in chile
gritan, our tongues gritan el derecho
                    gritan justicia;
and the forked ones encadenan
                en azúcares drogadas
twist our culture y envenenan
and the fire picazón boils en alientos
rapes melcocha mouths

to feed them lava
burning con chile la lengua
and the lies del arrastrado

DUSK DOUBLE DOORS

dusk double doors
    dirty cadenas of odio
    chained to the sweat shops
        the sweat fields and prisons
(outhouse omens)
open dawns of cold rushing,
rising in calvary thorns
freezing the spines of our pueblo
      nunca !! el colorado pueblo
      never !! nunca ...
in our barrio occupation is not allowed
let the barrio
    be a barrio, barrio, barrio.
barrio and not blood sweating colonia
planting cactus flower pots
regando el jardín de plumas
salute the sun in ayunas
mis labradores,
    carnales ... tear
    open las puertas de aztlán
    fuera del fil y de espinas
a proteger nuestras flores.

ASH WEDNESDAY CALAVERA

ash wednesday calavera
where the warrior eagles stand
    on the forehead
        no more ashes
    to grey dust
        no more our flight

to the solar god of war
                death incarnate
huitzilopochtli
cheek bones torn
worn down flesh
        once forgotten in the dusk
        staring from the dark
alone
        a thrusting truth of tripas
        flocked together
        bursting into birth
baptized with the thunder of cuetes
        in the spiral
(meditation — of a will to be)
alive
        to kneel before la raza
(burning flesh)
        and be blessed
in the death of eagled ash

EL DORSO DE DIOS

in the trepidous flight of a bird
        quetzalcoatl gave birth to its death
en las rocas
        las nubes morenas de su rojo sol
deslizáronse en agua
                miel y rojapiel
coloring its wool into skin
hicieron temblar los zenotes
                y los pueblos
y en las rocas quedó la emoción
        —el carnal de la cuatro
                        perdió su dolor
        por dinero cambió su color
                color miedo de lunas
                        cambió
                        por un sol
        y en el dorso de dios

42

el águila perched
            sobre isla y nopal
            víbora devoró
in the fall of a bird
            quetzalcoatl gave birth to its death

PACHUCO PAZ

we can all reach the point
            of knowing ourselves
to be mexicans in the north
mexican air with placas on walls
            names to be found
or carvings be read
            leaving no tracks
or marcas in the wind
music is born
            and la fiesta del silencio
permeates our hearts
and our blood pounds a beat
            to reach the point
where and when, rhythmically
            we know ourselves
to be
            chicanos de colorada piel
            de espíritu guerrero
hunting in our own land
            nuestra tierra

EN LA SELVA, ABANDONADAS

en la selva, abandonadas
            putrid tunas asoleadas call
gritan, gimen y se quejan
                del calor y de las nubes
waiting for the worms y lagartijas
sobre los nopales rojos

the stench settles in the wounded
the stench settles in the fog
y la soledad regresa al nido
el perdido encuentra su desierto
and the clouds bring shades and pensive shadows
las heridas de la tarde se desangran
    in a pestilent effort to be healed
agonizantes ante las flechas del sol
    llorando por la luna
        una
            tuna
    se pudre

A TRAVÉS DE LOS SUEÑOS

a través de los sueños
entre las necesidades de la carne
bajo los violados soles
i found a calpulli
warm tortilla plates of broken spears were served
    the palmeras staring at the windy passion of their
                    storm
and the children running naked en el callejón
    everybody was there y el espíritu de la
música
música, música
    sica sica musi
música de sarapes, de contrastes
    de cuetes y de cananas
en la sangre de mi raza rojapiel

A BONE

time
it shines with
a bone in one
hand
strange fate
dusty dreams
of immortality
of power
omnipotent
delusions
lost waves
rippled waters
trickling blood
hemorrhage
and death
killing time
it shines with
a bone
in one hand

MADRE TUMBA SOLEDAD

madre tumba soledad
    the fluttering of wings breathes papalotes
papalotl papalotl al sol ya vuelas
    on the string terreno que te jala
papalote encuentra tu razón destino
climb your cola de colores to the sun
skip the postes, slide
glide, papalotl, papalotl
    (gulp a crumb of leavened bread)
en tortillas calentadas serve your soul
bite the dusty bones of war and breath
    (break tortillas en tu comunión)
cut the venas of our blood and share
    crack abrazos and bring rain
where the tips of fingers touch

and hearts are caressed in clouds
where roofs de palma bring shade
los dátiles de ilusión crumble
sueños tighten bolts and drive harsh nails
              to devour las tripas of the wind
              lápidas rise
              to the sun of quiet epitaphs.

IT IS SAID

it is said
              that motecuhzoma ilhuicamina
sent***********
              an expedition
looking for the northern
              mythical land
where from the aztecs came
              la tierra
                    de
                    aztlán
              mythical land for those
              who dream of roses and
swallow thorns
              or for those who swallow thorns
      in powdered milk
feeling guilty about smelling flowers
              about looking for aztlán

MARRANA PLACA

revolution rape to mutate pigs
in the exasperated pangs of empty stomachs
kill for love of an angered freedom late to come
kill in yourself the oxide of your pestilent fear
assassination crawl to pigs and to those
                          running naked and afraid
mutant supper of aromatic exposure to the sun

46

like it is
tell yourself no lies, but sour truths
and sulphur boil for blood have for your nectar
mañana the thirst of drought and lacerated solitude
may swim along with you in death wish water falls
today, in the desperation of your cry sore throat
arid dreams can find oasis with nopales wet
razared be born to the cavern
to the obscurity, to the blackdark stench
razared be born
after your suicide mutation birth to quench
to the caverns bring a river crystal bath
to cleanse a pig
to rape a fear
to strip a lie and tell it like it is
in the desert of your sweat
the wetness of a tear add a bit of salsa
warm your plate
and of bones rid of en la libertad alada
fly with anchored heart to kiss an earth worm in his plight
razared be born in lungfull suck of dew
on fertile ground plow freedom
in the volition of your flesh
eat the frijoles off the palm trees in your islandgreen
partake of your bread
razablack, white, razared eat together
let the stare of pig grow blank
bland isolation he has reaped to die (alone perhaps)
the volition of our libertad has cried ya basta
to restore el pan de cada día
the pig will have to join our linda nación
to feed jorge, margarita, who hunger libertad

 *conejo*

TATA JUAN

if you see tata juan
con joroba caminando
speaking good english
 kind and careful
 and methodic
shuffling his body like a mountain
  rock of hope-now
   and tomorrow gone
jorobado se quedó
  ante los botones de su destrucción
playing with a máquina
  revisiting his childbirth
or working on his epitaph
  carving his tomb into tattooed cross
crucificado en la joroba de su jale
say to him
  carnal tu corazón palpita liberación
  respeto y hermandad humana
¡deja tu máquina chicano hermano!
  deja tu joroba y endereza tu vida
   tu cultura y tu razón de ser
caballero águila
  seguidor de las garras
   de la mano de bronce
if you see tata juan
dile que dios no es de lata, de fierro
  ni de aluminio
dile que dios es de bronce
  que guadalupe es tonantzín
y que san pedro es chicano

MADUROS HIJOS

la carnala y la carrera de san juan
en el anochecer de dudas y de miedos
san diego con sus rosas reza
guadalupe la madre, mujer-raza
madre de maduros hijos
pechos de rojizas carnes
corre, corre carnala
for we will grasp your palm
to stay, to live with us, mujer morena

ROLLING PEARL

in your eyes the sparkle of a dream
                    in vain
                    in solitude
you flow to seashore mother pearl
        perhaps the winter of your moon gloom
                    wet to drip
        to melt and bathe in pebbled paths
will find the strolling of a cricket lost
        in symphony to cry, to crawl away
                    to die but laugh
and laughter fill the freshness of your lips
                    your flesh to warm
embrace perchance the void
                    the chasm of your cry
the clamor and the blood to burst
        explosive butterfly to fly
in the host sand and foam splash
        your freedom find and hope
to walk again
        the tracks that you have inscribed
        to pass
to walk again your shadow cast
to tear the housing shell of tears
and find yourself to be
                    a rolling pearl

on blades of grass before the sun, a light
    the cavern of a gasping call
    in darkness never find your flesh again
but in the self of you a taste of loneliness
    an aromatic flight to kiss
a rib tide and a quiet stream
your smile

UNIDAD

    estamos juntos, unidos al grado que participamos
en cada una y otras vidas
en las vidas de cada otro
en las vidas de otro cada
en cada otra y unas vidas
en cada sol unidos in the darkness of
        our light
en cada soul juntos in the struggle of
        our national liberation
        together
    to the degree
    that we may participate
    in each other's lives
nosotros estamos juntos
    estamos unidos
pero no estados unidos
    el poder yace
    en el pueblo
    y no el estado
en nuestras manos la unión
en nuestras manos la junta.
    pa' celebrar la ocasión
    nos encontramos unidos
    es decir, juntos
    es decir
        estamos unidos
    porque la tierra
    es pa' todos
y no na' más pa'l estado yankee

COLD SWEAT

de vez en cuando
    la realidad del papel
ante mis ojos cristal
    en el dolor de mis palabras
descubro cavernas de oscuras sombras
sueños de madurez en rocas
    rocas rojas
    rejas tardes en la cárcel del ser
nunca, siempre
    acaso la importancia del ser
    calavera seca en el desierto
                desesperadamente
lloro, por dentro espinas
            arden las carnes
y la realidad se huye
        le pierdo en el sueño
        en la esperanzada fruta
        en la ya amargada tarde
se precipita el sol
    y la mar hierve de frío

IT IS

it is in the fundamental and ultimate interest
of our people,
of the people that would care to join our marcha
of an agrupation of red people that can
envision a concrete reality, and direct
resultant of our dreams to be brothers and sisters
in the blood
and in the spirit
    that binds us to this earth
and to the death that we can all
foresee as: inevitable decomposition
of our personalities as beings
of individual choice
of personal dedication to our claims

of this tierra
    as the one where our origins walked
    as people in society that have toiled
    as people in culture that have gathered
    as people in a human dwelling
across the bridge of time and legacy
aztlán is our tierra
    our nación
    our dwelling
    our responsibility.
we are not just being occupied
we are being allowed to survive
    under an illusion
an illusion that heavy on our eyelids
    believes in the omnipotent paternalism
of an angel sent from heaven
    to liberate us from the european oppressors
and establish the self determination
    of a continent that, from its inception
was cast in bronze
    and not in clay or ribs.
sickly we believe that the machinery
    through which we have to be
processed and departmentalized
is one that is parallel
    if not better
to the natural historical
    developments of the seeds of
the ones that have sweat blood
    on this land for millenniums
la máquina es un anacronismo
the bolts that bind it were
    not cast for our protection
or security but
for our safe keeping-out-of-the-main-stream
    mainstream of melted
elements to bathe no longer europe
    but the biggest white settlement
in amerindia, northamerikkka
el espíritu de liberación
    the spirit that thrusts us

to seek an opening, gasping
    for breath
shall inevitably be cast
    in respect for human dignity
and in due dedication to
    the nationalization of a land
where the rich shall cast
the jewels off their masks
and pledge psychologically, spiritually
    and materially the surplus
    of our toil to build
having chosen not to destroy
    the system which will bring
our people forth
        to be secured in employment
purpose and meaning in
    our historical calvary to the
liberation of our feet
        of our hands
        of our hearts
        of our minds
    and most important of all
            our fervent spirit to be
before the implacable machete
        de la muerte de los pueblos
that has presently infected the societal
        organs that oil the creaking
    socio-economic artifact of yankee society
and those who live under the influence
    clicking clumsily in the world of
        make-believe
    and close their-eyes-real-tight
        pa' arremedar a los yankees
what the hell for?

UMBILICAL CHALICE

the umbilical chord of my dreams
craves the marcha que mis padres engendraron
        in the chalice that
                once held
to be truly a pachanga
        el padre nuestro y guadalupe
                and the blood of the holy chalice
the time has come
        for all good men
to come to the aid of their country
        and to the misa de colores carnes
                simón que sí
                        que me prendan veladoras
                        que le digan a don juan
                que no permita el día
when i, blind
                fail to come
                        to mis carnales
                        to find the origins
                                the roots
                                the seeds
and the tears shed in the struggle
                to remain
the jardineros of our destiny
                to the soil, la madre tierra
in the vientre
        thimble, needle, cloth
thread doth?????????????
        do you dare carnal?
do you dare fall off the teatro
        the deception where máscaras are worn
and facades are painted every day to sell
        themselves
or the articles of their commerce
or the spirit of their blood
        the time has gone
                for all the space
        has not arrived
                for all evil persons

the itch
the witch
the ditch
    they all got together and you know what?
do you know what?
do you know what?
do you know what? no??????????????????
    well ....
        .... i don't either
because it was a bruja
        y la comezón de mi alma
that brewed the womb of ages
        where the men of barro melted into soil
and the monos de madera burned the sun con plumas
        where the man of carne y hueso
    traveled through by blood and brotherhood
    bearing a child of a witch
    itching to be in the ditch
        where the white witches once itched
la magia del corazón
        germinó en el espíritu
        germinó en el bronce
        y en el pueblo
in the umbilical dreams of my soul

FLORES PENSAMIENTOS

thoughts in words
        speak flowers
on the lips of men
        who pace time
to the disciplined pounding
        of a heart.
songs strengthen the path
        of he who has listened
to the wind tunnels that spray
        the lungs of love
        that blossoms truth
        naked before the sun

tearing the walls that secure us
to a world of our imagination
            the bird sways the thought
the wind and the night hover gloomy
            in their joy

SAPOBSIDIANA

sapos de obsidiana plague dreams
        and ametralladoras
aim sharp
        and shoot solitude
        in our pelos we can feel
the tremor and the blood
which many red people
have tried
        to drink
eyes in a taza de barro
in a plato de arroz
        como hongos feed on
the ashes of thought pursued
        and dreamt again
con la ayuda de un sapobsidiana
        de severa cara
                smiling

OFFERING OF MAN TO GOD

offering of man to god
        unwind
        unwind
        unwind the cord
the binding breath of earth
        of our umbilical history
        unwind
        unwind
        unwind the mind

that triggered shuts to kill
    and rape the path, bleeding
heart gasping into wilderness and sand
    a sun to see burn our fears away
    and bake our faith
    unwind
    unwind
    unwind your heart
into a trunk that offers music to the spirit
    and the woman of red flowers
offers melodies that trickle
    upwards to the flat topped pair of wings
that flap, flap, flap, flying to
the cloudy pillows of a dream
    of winds that wind
    around and upwards
    to the sun

THE PEOPLE BRONZED IN SUN

i'd be
    done, gone
razared, a long way a head
pero si nos vamos juntos
    venceremos el miedo y el abuso
we'll be long gone
we'll belong, gone our fears
    and the tear fertilizers of dreams
razared, i'd be done
    gone to my head the moon
when we want to reach to sun
    (el origen de nuestras quemaduras)
gone the sun
    orphan skins
would seek a father, a mother
    would seek the reason of our flesh
and the destiny of our

fearless
hearts daring abuse
to the people bronzed in sun

TURN ON

turn on
to your selves
'cause, carnales, carnalas
there just ain't
no carga
or righteous droga
as the self
that our heart bathes.
in blood rinsing
you can have
her strength
in you be shown.
slow down
look at your self
married to the bronze
that profiles our cheekbones
rising to the redsun's caress
and to the struggle of temples
in our breathing selves.

CLAY WATER

clay water
pulsating paths of pebbled rock
ages bygone of flesh
      molten   molten
   effigies flowing   in arterial mountain
ribs broken in angered flight of weaponed hand
        an ally
        an ally
     object of power's search for dwelling

59

                    lost to the pyramids
        gasping blinded yellow
                the sun and its daughter
                        tierra, tierra
                        continente
                        continente of dreams
                                of feathered heads
                        and songs of blasting silence
        red thirst
            breathing blood s
            bending backs or flexing chests
            breathing blood s
        barro breath
            dust jar of painted smiles

CHALICE

in the sceptered chalice
        the womb of solitude
and the blossoms of beating
        hearts, pounding — at once
in a path joined
        por la música sagrada
        en la muerte de miedos
juan persigue nubes
and skulls that spit
        births on palms opened to
offer flores
        "juan ...
                juan diego, corre
        derrama tu carne
            look at tonantzín
        en el monte de pétalos
te ofrece sus rosas
        la madre morena
en cáliz de bronce

HOT HUESOS

hot huesos
and war pending
    on the tearing of a jaw
chewing tripas
    pledging to the sun
a victory of hearts
    and fluids run
    down mejillas
y pómulos salientes
    guerreros en combate
madre tierra
    yield
    yield
    yield the fruit of
    ages
    maíz
    maíz
tripas gush in caldo
bones crack open
    guerra
    guerra
    grab, grab
bones of hunger war
    split heads
        and corazones
offer, pledge
    no more
    no more
blood cooked in oil
    veins plugged in grease
grease
grease
grease the gears
    machine bolts running
hearts betrothed
    married to the click
clack, clinging to the jaws
    suicidal grab

grab, grab a bone carnal
carnala grab a bone
and watch the warrior die.

ANTS, ANTS: CRAWLING

anthills climb through corridors
  run upward to the crater of the mound
  run downward to the heart of burning soil
corridors and labyrinths of heat
  sun rays flashing
  creeping spiders dead and gone
    carried, carried
ants of crumbful backs
and queens sit tight for flight
  to bear in womb
  more ants
and queens lay eggs to sacrifice
    and bake their wings
the sun, the heat and corridors
of angered crowds
  gathering dust, clamoring
    more, more
peace razared peace
  but when to see ourselves
now here, now gone
    in anthill climb
to find no thing
    no crumb, no heart,
what for the rush and bloody boil
  and pounding, pounding
clicking to our pace
  our selves now gone to hills
    in craters
      cracks and lonely darkness
  not a light
a step to follow gone to free
    ourselves to come
and bring forth backward

thrust of death and ugly
scars
        the earth yawns
while cave mouths chew away
and tremors fill our veins
            with gasping lostness
windy flight to burn
            and come again
to give birth bleeding
        sunbaked carcasses
in fat bellied
            hungry, thrifty
        crawling, craving
            climbing ants.

DAY AND FIRE

except those that crawl and fly were sacrificed
it was their custom to converse
        with their own hearts but
the wizards sought to snare him, quetzalcoatl
so that he would offer human sacrifices
symbols of his omnipresence were the
            other gods and not dead men
himself the scriptures and the wisdom
the plunge of a bird that rends
                itself; men are alive
"humanize their desires
        fortify their hearts
receive a strict instruction"
        tlamantinime
cáhuitl (that which is about to leave us)
like the night and the wind
is now here to stay in the day and in the fire

FACE YOUR FEARS CARNAL

do not ask of the sun
        to give no light
or ask the moon to hide
        her skirt of stars
do not torment your hearts
        and tear your faces
learn to live
        with the darkness
        with the wind
face your fears
die only once
        or a thousand times hiding
your face
        covering your ears
from the daring songs of your
        heart
hearten your pace into darkness
learn to live without
        asking your god
to be kind, gentle
        and to change; you walk
the moon will sing brighter
        in her skirt of stars and open your ears
the sun will color your heart and open your eyes

URBAN PRISON

la gorda de aluminum foil
arroz with corn and chícharos
        on top
presidio hill
        where the honchos
                on top
                        rule
                the time has come for all
                good men to come to the
                aid of their nation
and the ones

64

on the bottom in aztlán
struggle to breathe freedom
only to find
the bondage of the slave
in the skies covered
with clotting blood clouds
of smog bars and
dark chains of
factories smoking death
and coughing life in spasms

EN LAS MONTAÑAS

up the down ward
slope of valles
and cañadas
where rivers caress
the cheekbones of our meadows
and the sun comes
in ayunas mañanas
bañadas in mist
breathing water
falling to the ground
and maíz reaching for
the skies
we took peregrinaje
to the madre
sierra de montañas
con pinos
y bellotas, a veces
ardillas y carpas
refugio we found in
cuevas
pueblo indians nos
decían
while our doors opened
a little to see the pale envy of the yankee.

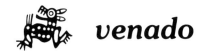 *venado*

BRONZE RAPE

la india se arrodillaba
    en el río,
a recoger agua iba.
    mujer de fibra.
bronce tez; apenas
        notables the round
    moons of her breasts
and hair dark; flowing
    to the breath and
will of ehecatl padre
    del viento;
y de la aventura alada
que prendió al criollo.
    en su bronceada caída
kissed her forehead
    and raped the silence
of the trickle, trickle
of the stream
    pulling the ground
to her red plumaje screaming
el mestizo
    ante el altar
nació sin padre
    pero sí con mucha madre

GOT TO BE ON TIME

time carnal time
    got to be
        on time mounted
riding yourself unto years
    of aging bronze
piel growing, ripening

67

            bursting into softened
                silken bronzed
            gold skin fathered
                by the sun
        aging now into arrugas
                turning la
        rueda de la vejez
                and time
        carnal, time, time
                clicking hours
        pounding unto death
                piercing silence
                piercing ears with time
                bound to
                time, redbrother
        time long gone
                time short coming
        time been walking dead
        the time has come
                to come
                to come
        to the aid of our nation
                aztlán
                aztlán
        land of sometime
                aftertime
        noontime, notime
                afternoontime, suntime
        alltime
        nighttime, moontime
                morning time,
        have atole con pan
        dulce y gordas
        con queso y salsa
                sometime land
        of our time and age
        of the fifth sun
                darkened
        with the smog of
        yankee rhythm machines of time decaying

CANDLE SHUFFLE

shuffling wax on
　　the pavement protest
of a vigil walk
　　on bishop's cathedral sleep
raza froze with
　　candles in hand
and fire in our hearts
　　whose cries died
in the thick blanketry
　　of the constipated sesos
in the bishop's calavera
we walked and talked
　　and sang and
argued but it was
palm trees and the skirt
　　of starry darkness
that savored our plight
　　pidiendo posada
en el nombre
　　del cielo
está encapotado and so
　　is el obispo
buenas son las nubes
　　pa' la lluvia
bueno es el obispo
pa' regar la sopa dreaming
　　while we hold
　　a velorio
to come into and share
his dreams
or to celebrate
　　his abdicated death
covered in black robe
　　con cruz
pendiente al ombligo
　　carga la
crucifixión en la panza llena
de sermones about
heavenly kingdoms for

the working poor
who are meek
    and give tithe
"¡10% pa'l señor!"
    ¿cuál señor?
¡el señor sacerdote!
¡la señora iglesia!
"¡¡el cielo!! ¡¡el cielo!!
that never gave us posada

BONES OF COURAGE

the bones of courage
    are with the máquinas
    the máquinas that bore
        the child of death
        hiroshima
        hiroshima
        hiroshima
    the human máquina
        from
        the
        laboratory created genocide weapons
    to protect their fragile
        loneliness
    their alienated minds
        lost
    without bodies
        sin corazón
        que marque sus veredas
    walking theories
        afraid to experience
                to learn with their bodies
                to breathe
                to pace our progress
    with the beating of our heart
pumping courage to our
                work
alienated minds

                    of walking theories
                    need to be awakened
                    torn from their dreams
                    and thrown
                    into their bodies
              to rot in flesh
                    or learn
                    to bear the
                        day and night
                    that crawls and flies
                    in the womb
                        of
                    mother tierra
                            tierra
                            tierra
                            tierra
                            tierra
                            amerindia
                            amerindia
                        call forth the sun
                            que suba el sol
                            que suba el sol
                            que suba el sol
                            que baje
        después
la oscura capa de estrellas
        después
la luna
        y la noche de vientos
                y cantos
                y sueños.
que suba la luna
que bañe la tierra
que perfume el vientre
        de la tierra nuestra
        amerindia
        amerindia
        amerindia
deja ya que crezcan
deja ya que brillen
        tus hijos

que brillen los hombres
en la oscura muerte
del alado miedo
padre de hiroshima
que muera
que muera la máquina-muerte
en los huesos
que muera en los huesos
y que brille el hombre
el hombre de amerindia
la mujer de amerindia
los hijos de amerindia
amerindia
amerindia
las hijas de amerindia
amerindia
amerindia
tierra de bronce
mestiza tierra
mestizos pueblos
amerindia
amerindia

TRÓPICO DE CEVICHE

a los orígenes de coco y palma
donde sentada espera
en su altar
the morning star
guaymas de tierra mojada
buenos días
sol
viajemos juntos
hawks sweep
clouds of desert dusk
mochis, mochis
m-sixteen clad
mexican soldiers

profanely sink
their g i botas
on yaqui ground...
no has llegado
a tus antiguas raíces, méxico
te añoran tus nopales
en tus madres sierras frías
and windy nights
sing by
against the yerbas
plucking melodies
        from puntas de maguey
    yaqui winds
    carve epitaphs with polvo
    on antiguas rocas
y jacinto dice
"pacencia raza,
        pacencia"
chavalitos, children
        roll to sleep on petates
    by el fuego
covered by our lady's
skirt of stars
    and surrounded by painted
desert darkness
    the silence of the cactus
            sings
no has llegado, méxico
a tus antiguas raíces...
    "polecía militar
    patrulla mazatlán y todo
centro urbano,"
    estudiantes explican,
        "intrusión del pulpo yankee
            estrangula
    tierra y libertad
        indígena
    tentacled yankee octopus
        arms pri's army
así
    la milicia mexicana

mantiene cuchillo al cuello
tepic, nayarit
    ojos de dios
te acosan en las montañas
    huicholes, huicholes
in manta pants,
    huaraches and rainbow colors
sarapes acinturados
    y campanas al sombrero
ringing paths of rhythmic melodies
    huicholes y coras
offer their hearts
    every day
to our father
    sol con plumas
and our mother
    tierra faldepalma
ya jalisco deja oler sus
    tierras rojas
mojadas plantas callejeras
    descalzas, sobre calles empedradas
    la raza en tuxpan anda
    cruzando el río san pedro
pa' la feria en rosamorada
pasos suaves encaminan
tropicales alientos y sonrisas francas
murmuran, rosamorada
amorada rosa
    pacíficas aguas
las faldas tropicales
uncover their coconut breasts
    fresh water
    rich oil for ageless
      skin
la raza mama
    la chichi e coco
y se protege del padre del tiempo
no has llegado
a tus antiguas raíces, méxico
    you are not from here
and you are not from there

74

you have no age
you have no future
you are not thirsty
nor is there any water
                go back
                go forth
rasca la tierra
busca el sol
everyplace, everytime
        lord and lady of the close vicinity
        navel of earth
        circle of fire
river waters
ocean waters
                mís maloya
                mismá loya
mismaló ya
        mismaloyá
sá lamandra mís maloya
salá mandra mismá loya
salamán dra mismaló ya
salamandrá mismaloyá
salamandra de los montes
mismaloya de los arcos
you have no age
you have no future
you are not hungry
nor is there any corn
                regresa
rasca la tierra
toca el cielo
busca el sol

EL CARNALISMO NOS UNE:
INDIO JUNIO SEIS

el carnalismo nos une
      y el amor hacia nuestros hermanos y hermanas
nos hace un pueblo ascendiente
la carne nos une
      en sufrimiento
      en dolor
en gozo, en alegría
los golpes y las caricias
los gritos y las sonrisas;
raza, raza, raza, raza
la pirámide de nuestro espíritu.
las raíces de nuestro corazón
      en las caras de los niños
nos recuerda la pureza destruida
      por la muerte ambulante
del yankee sin corazón
            sin dirección
            sin vereda
la vereda que nosotros, como pueblo, atravesamos
se ha encontrado con espinas y con tunas
      con monstruos metódicos y eficientes
con cárceles, con ejércitos
      con fábricas y con minas
con campos y con escuelas
      donde reina el silencio programado
por la máquina asesina
que idolatra a un dios verde, de papel
que compra cuerpos
      pa' trabajar en los campos, fábricas y minas
      pa' hacer guerra en amerindia, asia y áfrica
      pa' traer la misma muerte y dolor
que nos aqueja
      a las puertas del hogar en que habitamos...
¡muerte, muerte al perro de papel!
      el monstruo que le creo
      se atraganta con el sudor
con la carne y el esfuerzo
      de nuestro pueblo ascendiente

nos han robado el amor;
lo han convertido en moneda
¿cuánto tienes juan?
    déjame ver si te quiero
las murallas del miedo
    levanta el monstruo entre pueblos
entre hermanos que se acuchillan
mientras la máquina explota, mata
    mata y envenena
envenena nuestras venas
    con licor
    con heroína, con hamburguesas
con hot dogs, y aspirinas
    y desodorantes
que esconden el aroma
de los cuerpos que sufren
gozan, duelen
    y crecen con el amor
en las venas, en la carne, en los huesos
    raza, raza, raza, raza
el amor nos pertenece
nuestras canciones lo cantan
nuestra carne lo demanda
we love you carnal, carnala
jefe y jefa los queremos
el carnalismo nos une y
el amor hacia nuestros hermanos y hermanas
nos hace un pueblo ascendiente

GUERRA: PODER: PAZ —
UNA CARTA A TIZOC

es importante clarificar
    que el poder y la paz
se oponen el uno al otro sólo en las naciones
    que alimentan
    sus estómagos
con una economía de guerra
    que compite por los mercados

en la tierra traficando
usando y propagando
el narcótico del alto
y creciente nivel de vida
de los pocos en el mundo adictos a la guerra.
para los muchos...
el carnalismo es necesario, la guerra es obsoleta:
y la paz es otra fuente de poder
con violencia
faltan la claridad y el coraje
para actuar
a través de veredas de creación
cuando hay paz
en nuestro corazón, la única lucha que lidear
es en contra de nuestros enemigos naturales:
el miedo
la claridad
el poder
y la vejez
actos violentos para derrotar estos
enemigos naturales
de la especie humana
son actos suicidas
cometidos
en contra de uno mismo,
en contra de la raza
actos no violentos
tienen sus raíces en
nuestra tierna relación
con el coraje
y nuestro respeto por
el ciclo natural
de capullos florecientes
al marchitar de las flores al explotar de las semillas
de nuevo la paz extrae poder
de la vida y el sacrificio colectivo del ser
de los muchos oprimidos
la guerra está fundada y es mantenida
por la muerte y la explotación individual del ser
para beneficio de los pocos opresores
el poder y la paz

pueden jalar juntos
y perpetuar la familia
de la raza humana —
    nuestra
        madretierra,
            padresol,
y todos sus hijos vivientes
    nuestros carnales y carnalas
la hermana hormiga, la hermana abeja
    el hermano lobo
y el hermano árbol
la hermana flor
y el hermano maíz.

WHO ARE WE? ... SOMOS AZTLÁN:
A LETTER TO "EL JEFE CORKY"

a dog walks waggling
    its tail, proud
its chest out
    and its head high
another comes
    and fights him under the moon
tear all possible skin
    off each other
the first
    wins
and walks away in darkness
    having established power
through violent struggle, the other runs
    a month later
the dog no longer walks waggling
    its tail
another dog tears him
    ragged and fearful, the night before
with its tail between
    its legs, defeated, runs himself in darkness again
defeated by the people's
first natural enemy:

                    fear
the fear that all
        of us once face
before our christian ignorance
we see unknown evils/the devil or communism
        unknown feelings/the body or violence
        unknown thoughts/the mind or guilt
        unknown threats/death or god
        unknown pictures/dreams or nightmares
and we run, we run
we run, when we could walk, and see clearly;
without violence,
                we could walk
the path we all must walk:
        the path of peace, the path of peace
for those who want the power
        to impart life, knowledge, nourishment, and health.
weed out the paths of war
of those who exploit the power
        to bring death
and genocide
against one's self, the human race, suicide
        through governments
built with firepower
        and violent
military dictatorships.
in this country
                the united states
of (i beg your pardon)
                northamerikkka, yankeeland
general george washington
        became its first
commander general of the armed forces
        and its first
military dictator, president
        today, thursday
september ten
        san diego a.m.
before dawn break
        two thirds of every
u.s. federal tax dollar

80

is spent
on the military/for defense
we do not believe in suicide,
    or homicide,
    or genocide, or biocide
we do not wish to walk the deadly path
    of fear while living
we shall walk the path of courage
            and disciplined,
    defeat the people's enemy, fear, with nonviolently
    rooted power, our weapon justicia
to: establish peace,
    restore the earth,
    and respect the sun;
peace, earth and sun: peace, earth and sun
    can bring our
liberation from
ignorance, war, hunger, disease,
and military dictatorships
        be they white
            or black,
their violence must end
with our culture, our heart, and our peace.

YA ESTUFAS

espumado con atoles de nubes
            el cielo colorado
witnessed a dusk
            of murals
                painted
in the spirit
        of the fallen
brown dry leaves
        of autumn
las cananas en
        la tarde
aparecieron and
        thousands

of bullets
        turned
    to flowers,
kissed la raza's heart
            and many mexicans
cried "ya estufas
        viva la revolución"

SOLAR GROWTH

aranda's calavera
died silenced
        with chains
        trying to breathe peace
and his birth as
        a tolteca
    took its shape
in wood
in lacerated agony
        and painful
chips and chiseled
        birth
again guillermo
        flowered
and sung his
        heart's poemas
to the moon
        of his inspiration
and the solace
        of his
solar growth

TORTILLA HOST

a circle round
        the sun again
the pace of our pueblo
        del sol la vuelta
ha dado otra
        vez, otra nube
aparece la eterna
        tarde
tarde nunca llega el
        sol, al tiempo
explota y su piel se cubre
        de llagas
se limpia, se prende
        se apaga su sed
in the sacrifice
        que regresa
        que se lanza
a la vida solar
        y la tierra materna
espera fecunda
        fecunda
        fecunda la raza del sol
        as mountains
breathe el aliento
        de ehecatl pues
tlaloc en su rabia mojada
        has rinsed
of dust and of clouds
        la luz
morning, morning breaks
        in the playa mojada
and the ardent flesh
        quenches the pain
    . as the pebbles of sand
        in ayunas a star
brings salt to our lips
        moistened dawn
otro año carnal, carnala se nos llega
        nos pierde, nos pasa

y nos deja arrugada la piel
        longing
        longing for the freedom
        that hides
        in the shadow
we tear at our tripas
        in hate biting
our lips for its freshened caress
        time, otro año carnal, carnala
el setenta con uno se
        viste y nos deja
memorias y luces
        perdidas en la
oscuridad lápida
        del pasado/la muerte
nos pasa y la vida
        invita otra copa
did you see los espejos
        los reflejos del año
pasado de aztlán
        el primero
    el del grito nacido en el pecho
now llorando
now playing, now singing
        but crawling on fours
chavalito: la nación es joven
        apenas si el pueblo
se junta
        the nation has brought
to its nipple many
        muchos que maman
la chichi del movimiento sin
        ser hijos del sol y la luna
la luna los niega
        bastardos sin padre y
sin madre vagando en
        la noche de miedos
hay que velar: the movement is young
hay que velar el amanecer
        dawn is breaking
and the sunset builds

                    castles in wet afternoons
enero, enero
          el primero se rompen los jarros
clay is sacrificed
al año
          del sol encuerado
many sour fruits
          will flavor el año
del sol uno y setenta
          más su pueblo must face
               oppression
                    colonization
by the yankee empire
oppressed con hambre
          con ganas, con sed
          the colonized with chains
            en el corazón
          the razared
               of
          amerindia,
          our continent,
          clamors
            as
          liberation and unification
          pierce our senses
          smell/breathe
          touch the nipples
            of cornfield mountains
          and drums/move the movement
          dream a life
          live a dream
          cast off nightmares
          cast off fears
eat a plate of frijoles
          and rejoice in
               cebolla
let tortillas be host to your heart

ETERNAL TRIPAS

the átomos of
        our tripas, raza
                can fly
to the fathersun
        on motherearth's tortillas
gather your stones carnales
        get your canicas back
back, back to the flowing
                water causeways
of tenochtitlán
        back to the tears of tlaloc's agony
to the stillness of our sun
        ollintonatiuh, back to aztlán
        our son of movement
el retorno a la luz
        entre la noche y el día
                el grito de dolores
                despierta
                        la
                energía
        que no se mueve
en el rojosol del movimiento

MAR DE SANGRES

writing words
        to crack open empty silence,
and find nopales independientes
        con tunas carnes rojas
vivas. many a drop of rain
                has fallen;
over inflamed cheeks and
        dripping nosed chicanitos
                cough in los barrios
of dust. as the comal on our heart
        warms our blood and we play
                with our children round, and round

chicano man.
            hear the screaming, crying
wailing winds.
            all autumn leaves are flying
over the banquetas — junto a los yonkes
            de califas, arizona
                        new mexico, colorado
nevada, utah, texas, kansas, illinois.
                  junto a los yonkes
in every barrio there is a raza, raza
among the canneries/beyond the tracks
            some racist places hide the raza
                        of the land in dark stench corners
of smog and howling humans
                  freeze
            in the fields of profit
to the yankee clocked in christian time
                  shrouded with green money
      and shiny guns of frozen death
sabes que, carnal, carnala
            no me cae
      esta fuerza del yanki
            basada en nuestra muerte
            no me cae
la independencia
            nace en el corazón de
los individuos
            para florecer entre los pueblos
      bajo el sol
            en la tierra we walk
            en la tierra we speak
            en la tierra we love
            en la tierra we die
and find birth breaking
            in the mornings
chicano independence must dawn
            before economic progress
and the welfare of pockets
                  is filled; uncle sams
have anchored profit
            in the country's heart of coin

economic independence
        the movement of the pueblos
against dictatorships of money
        before our sun: ollintonatiuh
comes to the end of its cycle
        the strong in heart shall rise,
survive, and bear the burden of
        the weakened yankee minds
they refused to accept death
        and
        froze
        their
        bodies
        cold
        mechanic flesh
        of efficient immortality
        in ice; these shall
            melt
            before
            our moving sun
        now dawning
        carnalismo...
dentro de nuestro corazón
        blood flows at an even pace
and all violent rivers
    return to the calm
            of deep océanos
social change in uncle sam's organization
        band-aids wounds
y niega la sangre derramada
        en guerras
        nunca
        declaradas con
viet-nam, laos, cambodia
con el pueblo del rojosol naciente
        y manda raza
con pistolas y muerte
        then peace corps band-aid
rushingly the scars of war
    with good-willed uncle sam's
big brothers to be watched raping

bronze sisters.
in the stillness of our heart
        dedication can be found
to la causa
    la causa de toda esclavitud
    y muerte
con tierra y libertad
        ha de acabar/the burden
        the burden is ours
                raza
                raza
                raza
                raza
black, white, red
                raza
                raza
                raza
in our mixed blood
                all
                have
                come
                to
                be
                carnales
en el mar de sangres.

WINDLESS VENAS

guitarras tardes
        soleadas mañanas
como ríos corren
        los pensamientos
and the sea of theories
        splashes on the rocks of
established white wash shores;
        drowning brotherhood and sisterhood
once held in blood
        the tide of placas viene
tirando mordidas y pedradas miradas

wacha las aguas del río
wacha las aguas del mar
      todas calmadas regresan
toda violencia apaga su sed
      con los espejos del mar
         de colores sangres
derramadas
      las venas: our cause ways
are windless at sea.

GROW STRONG

entre colorados cielos
    the blazing redness of
      a sun
        now sinking
our flesh in the waters
our veins are refreshed
   in our struggle
   to be free to breathe
las caídas y ascensos de nuestro padresol
our father bleeds; smog clouds
        prevent him
from touching our skins.
      fathersun touch us with your radiant breath.
give us warmth
      motherearth weeps for your caresses
lost today in poisoned clouds
fathersun! come!
      brighten our faces
into gleaming bronce!
    carve pride on our cheekbones!
give wisdom to our heart!
   let us, raza, determine our path
   let us, raza, conquer fear amongst us
and in our imagesun
our flesh grow strong...
our bones grow strong,

90

our blood grow strong!
                    ¡carnal! ¡carnala!
our heart grow strong...!

SOLAR CLIFFS

entre rocas de niebla justicia
            nuestro padre sereno
                    se baña en la tarde.
se retira el abuelo solar en el cielo;
        and the winds, in their maritime breathing,
moisten nostrils of salted
                    caresses of freshness
to the stillness of time calaveras
            las olas...
            las olas...
marea, marea as our solar tradition
            cracks open the waters
the earth and sky in a fire flown sundown
well painted by sun reddened clouds
            oh! our father, be still!
stay with us on the path with a heart
            burning, stay, burning
            splashing, stay, splashing
                    in wisdom

DANZA LEONINA

zipping through concrete telarañas
            metallic ants turn to centipedes
and bright lights darken the ojos
            of one who sees the neon
and towers of smoking oil refineries
            of los ángeles muertos
muertos en la tarde de agosto
            the maíz was trampled by dogs
and many birds took flight

in the maze, the crying
cursing winds of northern icelands
in the summer
walk again on earth
and sing of peace and carnalismo
de raíces terrenales
proviniente de fecundo vientre
man stands and walks again
on earth
to listen with plantas descalzas
to the murmuring caress of
motherearth's latidos
she gave us birth in blood
and for the sun we have sacrificed
hasta los huesos tostados
en los desiertos de la incandescencia
del señor padresol
we have marched
migrated, walked the distance
of our lives in lonely stroll
below the moongloom of the night
as cherry headed armored ants wail
in the night of fire and smoke
splashing mud on sidewalk and walls
rushing to the hunt belly clubbed
gas masked, shot gun panting breaths
se chorrean de gusto de muerte
se chorrean de muerte de gusto
retiring at dawn to the beer canned existence
of idiot box stares, waiting
waiting for the prowling sunset of
another asphalt telaraña ride
riding over brotherhood
danza
riding over sisterhood
danza
riding over justice
danza
riding over peace
danza de plantas encueradas

danza de raza
danza de barro
danza de espíritu
danza de bronce
danza, danza, danza, danza

AQUÍ NOMÁS

as the lápida of our flesh
    all things once born on earth
    be gone ... aquí no más
    someday, someplace
motherearth devours her children
    and so she will
        me
        and
        you
        and
    we, sin embargo
where are we? ¿dónde estamos?
aquí nomás carnales y carnalas
    aquí nomás
    en la tierra
que como a sus hijos nos da chichi
    nos da maíz
    aquí nomás
    encontramos un sueño
our lives are the images we mirror
    while children
    on earth
we need not dream
    suicide, homicide
    genocide or biocide
our hearts must find our spot
    our place, our body
    our family, our tribe
    our nation and our motherearth
will welcome the return of her children
to her womb and our flesh

and her flesh shall be our dormant life
     again around our fathersun
     again
     again
     again
     again
aquí nomás en la tierra
     en la tierra aquí nomás

LEVÁNTATE Y RÍE

in the mud
    butterflies found birth
flying to the sun
    from the stillness of time calaveras
the eyes of all wrinkles
    come on to nopales
shedding their flesh in tears
    to the sun while on earth
las flores escuchan
    el canto del hombre
que penetra el silencio
como un niño que llora
    y que todo a la boca se mete
la nación se atraganta de miedos
y llora frustrada pues sus piernas
    le tiran al suelo
    y sus marchas no escucha ni el
    cielo, ni el sol
mas su llanto penetra la tierra
y la madre le escucha
    "aztlán, aztlán
levántate hija, camina, hijo
yergue tu espina y busca tu sol
    yo te doy maíz
no comas el veneno de yankee
    mastica, mastica
    tu maíz
hazme el amor, digiere mi leche

escucha el
latir
de mi pecho, escucha
descalzo
que tu carne es mi carne
eres tierra
hija, aztlán
eres tierra
que tu sangre es la sangre del sol
eres sol
levántate y ríe
que en tu vida
de espinas
la tuna se da
levántate y come
mama mi chichi, olvida el dolor
si tropiezas y caes
levántate
mama mi chichi, olvida el dolor
crece, grow
mama mi chichi, olvida el dolor
vuela, mariposa
vuela, you have crawled
enough
as worm
vuela, mariposa
vuela, you have slaved
enough
in chains
vuela, mariposa
vuela you have toiled
enough
with earth
vuela, mariposa
vuela, you will meet
the bearded redsun once again

DAWN EYED COSMOS

what if we wanted to climb
                    to the mountains
        and seek lakes of serpents
                    and eagles hunting
in the carrizales
            caña por suerte encontrásemos
y maíz plantásemos
            que la tierra fuera libre
y el sol brought flowers
            in the songs of our hearts
what if we lived
            with the tierra
treasuring the cracks in the sky
            of dawn eyed cosmos
        or sunset retiradas del señor/señora
do we want to go
        and blow up a building
        or can we change
the place of many
        pueblos heart
                    marching
        through the calles
cantando about nuestra
        nación
ofreciendo la vida
            a cambio de armonía
cantando de colores
            sarapes mañanas
"buenos días carnal, carnala;
        el sol amaneció con
nosotros
        y ha de partir en paz"
        the borders of all territories
        cannot last forever
"razared, you don't have to fix
                the fence"
        and uncle sam
            need
            not

kill
for
markets
and
cheap
labor
pools
we
don't have to slave or consume war's flesh
the thunder clouds
of our hearts
bring rain
to the smog of war:
and charcos
de agua temprana
flicker with the
face of quetzalcoatl
and the surrounding
eyes of night
let ehecatl/señor del viento
change the course
of our nubes
we need not
kill sam or sacrifice his heart
sam is suicidal
sam is killing himself
we need not
spill his blood
but then
we don't need to buy his death, or eat
his chemical replacement for organic life,
or sell ourselves
to his war of hate and fear and profit.
we can say
¡buenos días!
señor y señora
del cosmos ojos de amanecer
¡buenos días, corazón! ¡late!
late corazón
late y canta
tu canción

                    sing your pain
                        and pleasure
                            heart, give us
        your love unto death
                    give us
        your death unto love
        sing of the mirror
            and the face
        sing of the labyrinth
            and the heart
        sing of the dawn
            and the dusk
        sing of la razaroja
            and the cause, canta, corazón, canta

dawn's eye

1979–1981

'APÁ

'ace munchos años
treinta y tres para mí
i
sesenta i cuatro para ti
sin capa
toreamos
la vida
todos tus hijos
los cinco
i la seis
es presente
está ella, la única
preparada
no tenemos espada
tampoco
tampico
ni lideamos toros
somos aún
uristaheredia
doriabreu
    ¡i
    qué!
pos, tovía
    tiramos
ochos
al primer tiro

BALTAZAR

yo te conocí
a los diez años
con todo el genio
que tú ofrecías
padre
y tu motocicleta
en mil novecientos

cincuenta y siete
sorteando
    molinos de maíz

BEBO COMO PÁJARO

el águila
        tiene
    dos alas
    i
            vuela
            vuela
        ¿ve tú?
            ¿abuh?
    también
el tecolote
            buho

ERAN, HE RAN

            eran, he ran
irán i los días cesar
    del cuento, te cuento chávez
los helicópteros threading
    sombríos hilos
la venta de armas candled
    pendiente
    con jazz, sin monk
jimmi ain't no
    bautista boy, no peanut
    beheaded bow tie
teddi ain't no
    bear boy, farmer
    bochinche, boricua
transnationals

are not
into
democratus, brutus

Y TÚ LO SABES

y tú lo sabes por
                    todas las partes
          conocidas
                    regadas en vuestra
                    piel
          telaraña
                    vibrante tela
          de beso
                    que abrazo quiero
      dueño y
          señor
                    de tu cuerpo sobre
      mis ramas
                    compañera
                    compañera
                        de
                    corazón
        i qué
                    —no eres
                        extraña
        en mis
                    despertares
    huracanados

TAN

tan sólo tú i yo el mar
para soñar en el mundo
despertar de hijos amorosos
que grandes algún día serán
tan sólo tú i yo
podremos estrenar el cielo
el sol, la tierra, el mar
el trabajo familiar amor
la vida toca los amaneceres trinos
que nos despiden luego de la taza de café
no para siempre
pero sí para nuestra relación
recuerda vida
tocarme en la mañana
dejando la tormenta atrás
nosotros somos
uno
y dos
y cuatro
amor, alma, eres
gracias a dos
y yo soy el otro
mujer
de mi vida
corazón, bien sabes
cora y són seis

PAJARONIDO

en el canto
amor
ado, oda dada en
tregada a la ventura
        a la suerte
su sinceridad
ër sencilla
tea, té

pega la luz del sol
como
a todos nosotros
limpia, sin nube
        sin reservas
el amor prevalece
el amorluz
        florece
en nuestros cuatro
        brazos
        laboriosos
        cuatro
retoños, ojos crepúsculos
        al alba
la tormenta
        amanece
con el rocío
        del pajaronido

AZUCENA

azucena marilla calandria
en su piquito llevaba una rosa
de castilla, bañándose en el ur
en el urua, agua x clara ella
vasca luna, vasca tierra, vasta
y libre vasconia con cabello largo
y lienzo, y onda cazadora
con cuero riatado pa' tirar
piedra, roca, niebla, venado
en la jeta azul castilla
otra candela como tú no hay
a'nque la almohada, tu rostro
brilla voluntad y amor
... buenos días corazón
el cíclope gigante cae
azuza, azuza el toro azul
que ya la venada colorada
se remonta la sierra, con onda,

en guerra pinta sus cuadros
con roja sangre y alma cristalina
si nos dejas ahora en el lodo
nos traga españa y sus conejos
... o nos ayudas, o nos condenas
vástago vasco, regresa,
olvídate o quixotea el atlán, tico

PENETRA

"penetra mi cuerpo
como la lluvia penetra
            mi huerto
mi flor es tuya chuparosa"
            "chupaflor"
            hágase luz
hágase luz, ágapeluz
            peluznante lunaguadora
regando tuertos con ojo claro
            aguadora devisante
            libertaria copa de té
            plena lluvialivianadora
            dora
            adora
    vianadora
    vía
    alí
    alú
    ¿alah? ¿vía, ve tú el té? ¡bebe!
    llu (u' n' i) ... ¿y yo?
    a
    prieta
    prieta, apriétame
    tango ganas de un beso
    tangéame—toma dos (takes two to tango)
    amé y amo, aún, a'nque? pené ... ?

me hablas al oído
la humedad de tus labios
los verticales cruzados sobre mi muslo
y tus palabras timbran terremotos

xoo b do b do,   clink clink, tom tom
xoo b do b do   tom tom, clink clink
xoo b do b do   tom clink, clink tom
radio gonna sing all night, u know?

ya te lo dije ayer
que la falta de tu tez
niega a mi soledad refugio
amor mío
y mi pensamiento escapa
                    cora, acoge mi lluvia

ERES

como el colibrí en sus alas
creo en ti como en el volar
el trabajo es alotear, creo
en ti encontrarme y volar

        zapetas cambiando y platos lavando
        todavía atado a tu piel creo en tu
        aliento y el brillo de tus ojos risueños
        creo en ti, eres tú lo mejor de mi presente

eres tú mi otro yo
cabalgando "la mancha"
quixote y una espada
en la roca esfinxe

        la prisión de las palabras se
        regenera en los moriscos indios
        de corazón sonrisa luna llena

no cruces el río
si no puedes con la marea
recuerda que ambas orillas
acogen al ritmo de la misma ola

CON

        con
        salsa
        posera
    crismas
        quieres
    más, pepsicola
nadamás, gracias
        con
        o
        r
        a
        z
        ó
        ron

SLIVER

            sliver
        moondrum
            silence
        cross the desert
            dusk of
            sweeping hawks
                solitude remains
        the cave within
            above the rock
    sierras
        rattle snakes
and dance for
        the full
    blossom of
    dawn
        lunas

CHILD

child of august
    moonflowered heat
      summer's gone
again into the autumn
   wind
   wind rider lion
child of curled mane
    black   night
      starsoar
     fire
   lava cloud
child of the dawn
   zahi b u
what i, grandfather
and the
  sun
   b
gleam and hover warmth

    gorgeous ramble finding the barn
the haylofts rainbow straw woven caresses
thighs quiver to the staccato plucking of the rain
  ask the evening how the sun fell into the dusk, red
embraces that make me love u, the blues turn crimson

110

MAMA DON'T WANT U

"mama don't want u
    dadi don't need u
    momi cain't buy u love—"
                papi say, "don't
                give it up
                            babi,
i ain't lying on a bed of roses
                mija"
                ... said he
        melancholia
                la serenidad
        nuestra
                vida amorosa
                    de suspenso
    somos una   sola
                herida
            wounded in
        the rhythm of our breath
                    never,
    however,   a very long word ...
                though
                    u
                    seem not too absolute

IXTOC

                all over
all over the world
        ixtoc speaks of the elder bones
perhaps of the first human race
        and its brethren giants
plants and animals
        "b some body and speak forth"
the hummingbird hummed
        and the world listened
as houston's shores gazed
            in awe

111

to the spill
and el paso
witnessed the exodus and the pride
and the perseverance in labor
in the production of wealth
with limited returns
the people choose to stay
and paytaxes
driving junkyards off
out   of the barrio's borders
—the real borders—
people versus junk
junk versus flowers and songs

THIS OL' WORLD

this ol' world some time too much
in front of the children
the selling of bombs
an' talking 'bout
kon, con
trolo
trol an' truk
truk 'an trol, roll
no nothing more
than what
"u willing to buy"
even at the sum mit
the palestinians
are hesitant
at caressing up
holy wall glove
what is the begging that must occur
this old world wonders
'bout the foot u
r, yeti
without the luxury
of
oil

                or
                    guns
                    and
                    tenichoose

'TILL I

'till i hold u in my eyes again
                    u remain imageless
it is only your symbols, your jests
                    which keep u real in my heart
i can only smirk
            my smirk is gone
                    without u
there is no laughter, or song
                    or flower
                    without you
        there is only darkness
                    and the real escapes me
                    i dream
                    and i suffer
                    and i long for u in deep sleep
                    making sure u
                    r
                    there
                    with me
                    on the loft, left
            and the sandalwood burning

ZAMNA

"sleeps in the morning
            don't know when to rise"
children's   babble hovers above the loft
            his   thoughts wander
            still
            on   the land

```
                    travelling, breathlessly
          through the morn
                    that comes and goes
       in sales slips
                    occupied
                    with asphalted parking lots
       and property taxes
santana's high noon winds boil the breath in l.a.
                    thinking 'bout the times
                    the times frolicked in the fields
                    of grass and corn
                    and avocado trees
                    and eucalyptus giants
              he
                    sleeps after waking
                    on to daily exercises
                    on to daily contemplations
... revolution is still a     solid daydream
```

ZAHI

```
sing of love
sing of reason
        splash a tear
    before the babe
              the one that babbles
              wonder
              and sparkles love
              in the wisdom
              of his iris
              his eyes light up
              and his brows arch
an arrow portrait of my path
              his smirk rainbows
              the colors of our kiss
              your lips remember rain
              and the pool tables full
              as munchies wabble
              cooks fry rice and boil
```

the beans with laurel leaves
the spinal bow is taut and willing
to be born, death itself is boring
waddle an ocean
learn to love me best of all
learn to tango garlic
towards life's tan gulfs

THRU OUR WINDOWED LOFT

thru our   windowed loft
we wonder 'bout the sprinkled grass
the blades forebode the morn
the morn that brought
our thighs
together
to
gather
our
selves
in
one
breath spread
in
one
belly
button

FREE

free as we are
from the bondage
the age of bonds
remains a buy
and
a twenty year sale
why should we b

                    afraid
          to love
                    in spite
                    of the rape of words
               love   inside
                 re   mains
                    with the flower
and the song twangs the guitars
          the plucking blooms upon the cactus
as   the drum drums chants and clouds
                    gather
grandmothers water weeds
                    fruits burst forth
                    work is wealth
our sweat is sweet
                    our honey, labor
               us, b's — we is

to show my heart
          a dance beckons the column
indian buffalo   herds
          hoof the dust of diamond heads

REBELLIOUS CLOUDS

rebellious clouds foster
        unwarranted rain
the dams do not, cannot hold the pressure
      the people, flooded
            flee
       and the rivers overflow
wanted: dead or alive
        raindance drummers
    reward
      re
        ward
        wa
        wa
        ward
        wa
        wa
      re
        volt

WOULD U LIKE TO

would u like to
      sing and wordweave
         melodee
     teach u
       how
    2, too, two, tu
      sing & dance
         tango
         fandango
     for a dime
       without
       mine
       lost
       fore
     songs
       b

gun
　　　harmoni's an open
　　　breeze
　　saw, weave, sew
　　　sow what thigh reap
　　　u
　　tell　mi
　　cause　i tronó

chuck　the asphalt and the nukes
　　　strategic arms talks
　　　　　are drenched with mexican oil
corn prevails

BREATHE

breathe
drink
eat
think
　　　　b subjacent, scent
any thing, one, or body
　　　in thee world of tonal
nahual personified in functions
to b multiple
once must b five

```
            at least
        scent
              erred
        balan
                ced
              love rhythms
and zygotes swimming
                  past
        the mire
```

BYE

```
bye then,
    it would've been strong winds
                    by then
                i look for doors
                  as walls rise
and establish themselves
                    as borders
                    not shores
        electrified fences, not rainbows
                    and helicoptered moons
taught well to pursue demons
                    cockroaches
                    and skunks
              even ants
                    and bees succumb
                  to the onslaught
                  ... temporarily
        u and mi, me?
                    broder
                    sister
                    nos
                    and
                    otros
              remain one, and mortal
```

SUBWAY NO WAY

subway no way
            for good   moon
            to go
        down on an uptown
        train
                let me b
                thy guide
espan
ish
har
lem
    never grow no seeds
                in newyorciti
            praise the people
                that survive
        through the night
                and slush
                and mud
                below zero
    without coal
                bless the
                quilts
            that
        grandma wove
back in carmen city, campeche

PUT DISTANCE ROUND

put distance round
            found look see
                dancing
        satisfied claiming
                ground
                    beyond l.a.
        southbound
                and well rooted
            in the child's

```
          demand
                    for corncakes
     flake         naught
                    the morn's
                    raisin
     and           pecan bowl
       feeds                    hungered
            avocado dreams
                         shrouded with coriander
                    kisses behind the ear
          silently
                    while the sandpiper
                    slurps dawn's worms
```

TIME THIGH NIPPLE

```
time thigh nipple
          woman
          man won't
          disturb
    count enance
      or bodi
     holi
          li
    whole woman
    sleep
          ing
       no
          angst
       but
          love
       re
    main
          one
       in
          two
    sin thee
          sized
```

ROUND MY, ME

round my, me
                    i
        woman, she
                comes
        and sorrow my, mío
                solo yo
        espero
                veriyoung
        up to
                thy sky
        good
                bye
        what will u
                leave us
                            'ora
                    no cause
                to think
                    that i
                won't stay
        when u think
                    wrong of me
                    i
                    is left
        for u, onli

TALONES, PAÑALES

talones, pañales
                hijos
        porque'l
                            amor
        caliente
                on the tears
        tear the rain
            of dignity
                never
                long too much

122

```
                    a word
                       u
        none the less
                      is
                      me
                      o
                      c
                      is
                      u
```

FRIENDS ABOVE ALL

```
friends above all
            whenever thee onli one
                        cries to share simple
                        joys an' pains witch u
            friend 'bove all
                        or nothing
                    if ab
                    solutes
                        b
                        dealt witch
            crawling i learn to fli
                        i, thee worm
                        to spell
                    a thought, feeling
        sentiment, gnotion
                    ma._.? ná? ... ! ná?!?
            rrow lettered fri
                crisp, fri
                        ends cross
                                cut bow
                arch friends, arch
                        be
                        yond
                        cobras?
```

walking in amsterdam's streets
        through the warbles of its dawn
children catch the metro to learn history
        in english and dutch

the sun is shining
        truly
brick houses and clouds
    have taken its light
      hostage

the snow will wait
      until the crescent moon
slivers the   eve's dome

calexico quivers, rattles
        past sunsetting winds
amsterdam longs for the warmth
        of a southern california crepúsculo

dutch in the city squat
        and fight off guards
rent goes unpaid and flowers blossom
        on windowsills

DO U

do u remember
the parody of trembling laughter
through the parks clouded by moonlight
                    shadows, do you remember
                    the rain
        and the thunder
                    mushrooming
                    huracanes
        do u remember
                    under our feet
life sprouted on wet dark
                    earth, do u
                            remember
        the dew of dawn lightning
while our guts tightened
                    the irony grew
        out of asphalt
                and found its
                way into
                neon
            celluloid
        and vinyl cuts
                of memories
        running amok
                on wheels
        burning dinosaur bones
and some roaches
        rolling down a '47 chevy

THEN IT IS A PRISON

then it is a prison
go
forth, find, fiddle
forget u'r tro-
balls bounce
all i can say

126

don't let the bars
steel u'r vertical movements
el moro, moorish mariscos
mariscos, shelled fish
off moroccan coasts
dusting urbanity on woodened wheels
ellos, them git
git años together in kundalini cante xondo
zapateado, booting sports through the rain
sparking leathered cruise cross the flooded plains
whirling with hurricaned breeze
spraying ocean moons and bleeding hearts
leap to the moment full, doe is fertile womb
the tide gathers and sharks are cast 'gainstone
'nbroken, jaws 'n fins float lifeless fore the storm
after
all
is
steel
that remains ...

WITH

with out u darling, ling, sling
                shot to thee heart
locked up in blues, ling sling
                shot centered
                on the toes of a
                twirling turn
                yeah! yeah!
                for u, oh girl
                do it, duet one more
                time cain't git
                    e, nough
                    ee, nough
                    i, nough
            o'
            u
            babe

                    gulp culp
                    writ hulk
                      pulk
                      e, ē
                      i kē
                               corazón
            heart i
            still dia, dia
               logue, logo
            with u, xé

RAGING

raging rain rattles gutters
condominiums sway
ocean spray rustles
frogs croak spring blossoming
a dynasty is anew yin and yang

FIRE AND EARTH

tronó where i gonna go when the volcano blow
mon u better wach your feet
¡lava burn mon, lava hot!
better love me now before volcano blow!
din't wanna land in the city ...
the dump ... the junkyard ... don't wanna land
nowhere where u is not
wanna land in your forests, your peaks
your sighs and moans, your thighs and thoughts
tronó where i gonna go when the volcano blow
mon u better wach your feet
¡lava burn mon, lava hot!

NAUGHT

it's best to b
and b in love
and b not otherwise
wisdom has no room
for indecision
love and b! ...
or love not
and b that
which u are not
—imagine at least,
assemble the semblance—
and boogie
and bogart
naught

ASTROBIOGRAFÍA

in the beginning there was a lion
who met a goat who begot a liongoat
who mated a fish who begot
one like her and an eagle
scorpionserpent and the mind was missing and fire and
earth and water invoked the water bearer to let the human
show itself and aquarius was manifest and with liongoat
begot the moon and an infant sun.

GO TELL

go tell an easy soul
to be asphalted
halted on its ground
find no decaffeinated
no, no nicotine
no, no cocaine
kitchen woman

no more, war is
pending on the tip
of a broken feather
no, no more
not again, the drummer
shall, will survive
pounding on his skin
her bosom in dreams
and children marching
with their hearts
with their minds
stand naked
before the sun
i hug and treasure
no more war
if necessary now
we kill, we b born
     we is

PEOPLE ASKING ME

people asking me to dance with a fix, now, know no
nothing tell u horse, i ride nonethe park no fool horses
young wild and winning could b my friends there is no
fortune sugar zombi sugar enemy that can cut my sleep
in two thru the coals and lemon slices see the door step
no gutter stutter not no welcome for the sinner ayatollah
b u gray, white bearded koran, bible lord, krishna crouch
cross legged ready to fight bah, bhagavad gita a sword
is ours after all an' war remains an internal thoughtdream
no nightmare, mare, mar my dinner i cook it 'n' i wash
my dish. i cook not for myself. i cook for us cora, zón
zón. zón. cora. zón. sleep at the wheel burping and
bumping into police cars frozen in their black and white.
i freeze, freeze? with thought and dreams and pillows and
cigarettes and morning coffee. ragged and tenishoed
cross the chino snow the vikings listen to the mayanano,
nano, parked above the roof. lofty bleeding without
bogart, cagney or pacino. alive. haciendo la lucha

solito, alone and in good company. reservoir memories.
eyes. ankles. manes. and. and. and. the children 'till
running without shoes. people know naught revolution
is somewhere awaiting to be awakened lovingly and
mercilessly a time some day a time for us together to b
learning and turning wheels overturning tables forgiving
the foregoing blessing of a candled kiss hold my hand
there is a place for revolt and humanity to meet off the
street, i dream crosslegged foursome on our loft. i dream
of peace. i make and battle the cold morn. coral, pearl,
turquoise, silver and gold. spine. spine.

SUNDAY DESPERADOS

sunday desperados past san dementes, clementes steel
north, south crossing lines passed forged cigarettes
worth their salt and lemon blues not with a new baby
waiting in sacramento, now i ain't no senator saturday
night live and museums exhibiting gold while your hair
is parted and lovely is a trite word for thee and i, thighs
that know each other with a smile a teardrop off a eu-
calyptus leaf minty boulevard who knows naught but a
couple of cubs roaring colors cross the mire, cain't b
too true when the town disowns thy face shave and
shingle father of night, grandmother moon sliced for
thee, i, one who votes naught, not no realtor or elephant
man, know not no nothing off the street telescopes
saturn wears many rings who jog heartily even though
wounded heretofore writ, habeas corpus, git me out,
out of this here therefor idol of memories no talking
tongue, no tomato no potato, no plato, socrates committed suicide driven to the parthenon, cheers. it is a
choice. i am on the road. solar plexus sky bound to love
u cross the tulips 'n' carve countenance out me walk
sparking sparks off the preparedness of an old man
bearded and concerned which, witch, with? what? is to
be done. shave lenin, trotsky won't survive, stalin and
khrushchev prevail. ho. ho. ho. chi. chi. min. sunday
desperados still playing roulette in saigon. and losing

only once. the deer hunter don't go killing no thirteen
horned beast. moving violation cross the woodland.
deer. o. how i treasure the musk of your vertical lips

NETHER, NETHER, NETHERLAND

nether, nether, netherland coffee cups imported from
taiwan and main china marbles slung against the windmills
they slinged shot rhythm upon the wooden gliders off the
viking cliffs kirk douglas hath no horns upon his casket,
bronze basin cast his head the rowboat hath its slaves
before the steam boating is now a skim the water pastime
in florida speedboating sabotage off independent islands
huracanes rage towards the gulf of mexico snake head
península yucateca, the mayalo colora spine in chiapas
flying saucers dance with automatic machine guns and
mashhatters patch up the wounded to return them to the
nether, netherland of the fuggers or was it faggers,
fuckers? fockers? anyway the family that funded st.
peter's cathedral's mural completion, what ever hap-
pened to mecenas?   ... mecenas went to disneyland.

2 B DONE

lenin died sixty
three years ago
on down i now
wear a tie
and shine
boot out the
fascists and
the nukes and
shuffle over
flowing daze
days, months
... a monkey
got elected

what we gonna
do 'bout his
peanuts and
banana chi
quita panamá
po' no nuclear
welcome no
more mornings
no more
melodies or
hometown
blues, time
high to rise
and b one
    2 do

PLAN

plan to see the morrow
through the penumbra of other ones
a state of mind, a state
an order, maker never mind
make up rainbows shooting stars
crossing arrows thru one heart
borders melt their fences clockwise

FROM AMSTERDAM

no lo creo todavía
debo estar soñando,
hablando en español
escuchando a silvio rodríguez
en casa de arie
en amsterdam
no lo creo todavía
debo estar soñando
el sol no ha salido todavía
es la una de la tarde
debo estar soñando
en amsterdam
en español son las cuatro
de la madrugada
en realidad es un mundo sólo
sólo uno y somos todos humanos
y nos duele lo mismo a todos
a rembrandt lo enterraron
aquí y aquí anne frank hizo
su diario tito puente toca
hoy en la noche mientras
el cuarto tribunal bertrand
russell enfoca con su lupa
holandesa sobre los derechos
de los pueblos amerindios
ayer fue día de gracias
los indios trajeron pavo
ha llegado la hora del granizo
la nieve es inminente ayer
comimos caldo de lentejas
y bebimos bordeaux de lo
más rojo, más rojo que el
propio socialismo los poetas
que quedan comparten pan
y el frío penetra los ladrillos
en una rosa amarilla
anoche he visto el rostro de
mi compañera sus pétalos
sonreían a la media noche

eran sólo las tres de la tarde
no sé cómo la pluma negra
de cuervo que me acompañó
invocó a aquella mujer
que edgar allan poe había
perdido vino volando de
yugoslavia a decirme que
el socialismo no era una
teoría sonriente y con
chispeantes ojos me acarició
con una lengua bien extraña
a mis oídos luego me dijo
en perfecto castellano que
de la frente me brotaba el sol
no lo creo todavía
debo estar soñando
en amsterdam
en español es berlín treintaiséis
debo estar en la ciudad
de méxico en la casa
de mi abuela lola con sus
escaleras de caracol y su
tragaluz alumbrando el
ascenso al apartamento
cuatro debo estar soñando
en san diego en español
en austin debo estar soñando
treinta personas miraban un
turco ahogarse en la mierda
de un canal y más de dos
se echaron al rescate para
salvar a un perro no se sabe
porque vale más "el mejor
amigo del hombre" que el
hombre mismo acaso el
hombre no ladra a la luna
y el perro marca los ciclos
terrenales sobre los mosaicos
urbanos que el turco bien
no camina y tropieza
debo estar soñando en

español en amsterdam
me miran como turco,
suriname o indonesio
cuando bien soy amerindio
chicano moro maya con
salsa de país vasco los
taxis no me hacen caso
y me empapo en el
racismo de holanda
ni las prostitutas nos
ofrecen sus ombligos
no parecemos turistas
víctor, pedro y yo
ayer salió mi foto en
el periódico nacional
hoy no salgo a la calle
voy a contar los granizos
a preparar el derrame
de vocablos glifos rojos
de sentencias sin frontera
voy a contar los granizos
y los chevrolets que cruzan
la ciudad huele a ajolote
el croar de las ranas
surge del desague y
los canales con puente
no lo puedo creer estoy
en shelter island en el
half moon inn wachando
un documental sobre el
derecho al aborto basado
en la voluntad femenina
no lo creo, no lo puedo
creer aristóteles recomen-
daba a la mujer encinta
que desease una niña
acostarse en su costado
izquierdo, los plátanos
fueron recomendados también
las espermas o esperma-
tozoides o son y (griega)

o son x sin embargo es
un hecho histórico y bien
corroborado que después
de una guerra nacen
más hombrecitos y
medio mundo se encuen-
tra encinta ¿será el
útero caliente o el rebo-
zante pene y su leche
guerrera? ¿será la pólvora
en el aire? ¿será yin-yang?
los espermatozoides "y"
nadan mejor que los
"x" cuyo vigor es menor
habrá que preguntar
al maestro anaya tal
vez hinojosa sabe sin
embargo ruíz y esparza
han capturado la luz
tal vez ellos me saquen
de este apuro, que en
realidad no me apura
pero el documentario con-
tinua inevitablemente
arrastrando pico en flanders
pa'ca come here pa'ca
bro', aquí nosotros somos
uno, indivisible con todo
y el punk, el leather,
y el zen ginsberg me
cayó muy bien, personal-
mente, digo 'ora que ...
podíamos platicar sobre
su obra y preguntarle
a kerouac en su tumba
si louie armstrong usaba
lipsaver o monk ivory

RETURN

return to roots
revolt the gears
of this here death
machine gunned
future shock in order
to deliver us
to a brave new world
through technology
and the extensions
of our selves
and wills removed
once to reappear
within our selves
appendages of our
once extensions lost
in the chaos without
within joyous lakes
outwitted owls
of nightly clouds
howl unbending revolution

bibliography

BIBLIOGRAPHY OF WORKS BY AND ABOUT ALURISTA

Ernestina N. Eger

Alurista has become, since his first publication in 1965 (see item 85), one of the most popular and influential poets of the *floreci-miento* of Chicano letters. Tomás Ybarra-Frausto notes Alurista's "emphasis on poetry as spoken rather than privately read" (item 135, p. 118); some recorded performances are commercially available (items 182-85). In addition, his publications have grown from early inclusion in *movimiento* and counter-culture newspapers and little magazines to frequent anthologizing, five book-length collections, and the coeditorship, with Xelina, of the literary journal *Maize*. Critical analysis of Alurista's work has ranged from reviews (items 142-49) to a thesis and parts of several dissertations (items 136-41). Important to future research is the archive recently acquired by the University of Texas at Austin (item 181).

This bibliography attempts exhaustive coverage of print materials concerning Alurista. His works are subdivided by genre and type of source; they are alphabetized by title except in sections C and D, groups of poems which are listed under the title and date of the journal, magazine, newspaper, or anthology that published them. Works about Alurista, subdivided by type, are alphabetized by author's name. Unseen or unverifiable items are indicated by an asterisk.

Por su valiosa ayuda en la compilación de esta obrita, les hacemos constar nuestro más sincero agradecimiento a Beto y Xeli, a Angie Chabram, y a Richard y Ann Chabrán.

I. Works by Alurista

A. Poetry collections

1. *A'nque* [: *Collected Works 1976-79*]. San Diego, CA: Maize Publications, 1979. 63 pp.
   Incl. " 'taba," "los," "la mire bailando," "ama," "dadores de la vida (pa'juan-felipe)," "si le canto," " 'taba, 'tabá," " 'ora," "fascil," "después," "travesiaustin,"

"tuna," "acaso," "a," "a'nque," "con," "cabezeando," "sin," "igualda' tecata," "moisés come caca de toro," "mojologue," "así," "pués," and "clavado."
  2. *Floricanto en Aztlán*. Los Angeles: Chicano Cultural Center, Univ. of California, 1971 & 1976. Preface, Juan Gómez [-Quiñones]. Introd. to 2nd edition, Roberto Sifuentes. [112 pp.]
  Incl. "when raza?," "la canería y el sol," "I can't," "the man has lost his shadow," "libertad sin lágrimas," "hombre ciego," "la cucaracha," "las canicas y mis callos," "chicano heart," "el sarape de mi personalidad," "me habló en el sueño," "you know that i would be untrue," "tú sabes," "oppressive chains," "you have seen the cucaracha," "in the barrio sopla el viento," "bendito sea tu vientre," "el maguey en su desierto," "what's happening ...," "we walk on pebbled streets," "el buho sabio de mi aldea," "la música en mis venas navega," "we've played cowboys," "tizoc nos legó su pelo," "address," "must be the season of the witch," "la casa de mi padre," "my sister," "with liberty and justice for all," "unexpectedly," "I can see reality," "wheat paper cucarachas," "the rocking chair," "a cualquier hora," "el patriarca de mi pueblo es el amor," "en el barrio," "el león ruge," "jimi hendrix," "flowers in the lake," "mis ojos hinchados," "la carne de tus labios," "i know what awaits me," "i found the world outside of me," "de dignidad," "the sand i sip," "la pluma de mi vejez," "on the couch a can," "en la mesa," "el carpintero de mi destino," "las tripas y los condes," "pómulos salientes," "el pan nuestro," "fruto de bronce," "chicano infante," "fingers snapping," "los ninos crecen," "sacred robe," "Once, I wrote a Letter to Emiliano," "midday break," "take you down," "others in the quilt," "skinprints," "nuestras indias," "lick the maze," "to be fathers once again," "cat walked in," "elegante porte," "el recuerdo de mis grillos," "cuervo chicano," "bendita suerte," "grietas paredes," "moongloom dreams," "cantos de ranas viejas," "los poros de mi piel," "bosques," "insane buildings," "en el núcleo se pasea la mosca," "the anthills i climbed," "aurora matutina," "entre frígidos rangos mi pueblo hierve," "lanchas carnes," "me rehuzo como el buho," "allá ajüera," "lava brota de mi raza nopal bronze," "in true hostility have i found you," "the homeland of my heart," "nuestro barrio," "it was many minds ago," "coins on wood," "i found a picture," "la lechuza brama fuego," "something coming on," "brother man," "i've been conditioned," "raza ain't you tired," "tarde sobria," "los nopales con espinas carnes," "man thinks you just began it," "the man say we making noise," and "can this really be the end."
  3. *Nationchild plumaroja: 1969-1972*. San Diego: Toltecas en Aztlán, 1972. [196 pp.]
  Incl. "we would have been relieved with death," "salsa con crackers," "i have found my flesh," "construyendo una balsa," "spitting the wounds off my fire," "chicano commencement," "piedra roca niebla," "barriendo las hojas secas," "ride bycicle paperboy," "death riding on a soda cracker," "when you have the earth in mouthful," "carnales el amor nos pertenece," "evenflo bottle feed," "cuando la cucaracha camine," "by the gentle flapping of a palm, on the steps," "taza de barro en la que bebo mi café," "let yourself be sidetracked by your güiro," "i like to sleep," "thinking is the best way," "heavy drag street of smog," "tuning flower tones," "because la raza is tired," "walking down," "tal vez porque te quiero," "through the fences that surround you, grita," "built-in chains

vacations paid," "juan diego," "born in the steps of a desert," "me retiro con mis sueños," "mi mind," "tus dedos la tierra cubre," "come down my cheek raza roja," "coco, coco," "i had chilaquiles," "before the flesh in bones," "nuestra casa—denver '69," "a child to be born," "blow up tight to fly," "los tambores, los tambores," "la calabaza is gonna," "we can work it out raza," "down walled alleys marked," "out the alley our soul awaits us," "tal vez en el amanecer," "las cananas y el calvario," "labyrinth of scarred hearts," "clamped almas," "criollo you lived prohibition," "corazón lápida," "lenguagarganta acallecida," "dusk double doors," "ash wednesday calavera," "el dorso de dios," "pachuco paz," "en la selva, abandonadas," "a través de los sueños," "a bone," "madre tumba soledad," "it is said," "marrana placa," "tata juan," "maduros hijos," "rolling pearl," "unidad," "cold sweat," "it is," "umbelical chalice," "flores pensamientos," "saposidiana," "offering of man to god," "the people bronzed in sun," "turn on," "clay water," "chalice," "hot huesos," "ants, ants: crawling," "day and fire," "face your fears carnal," "urban prison," "en las montañas," "bronze rape," "got to be on time," "candle shuffle," "bones of courage," "trópico de ceviche," "el carnalismo nos une," "guerra: poder: paz—una carta a Tizoc," "who are we? ... somos Aztlán: a letter to 'el jefe corky'," "ya estufas," "solar growth," "tortilla host," "eternal tripas," "mar de sangres," "windless venas," "grow strong," "solar cliffs," "danza leonina," "aquí nomás," "levántate y ríe," and "dawn eyed cosmos." Rpt. in this volume, pp. 1-98.

4. *Spik in glyph?* Houston, TX: Arte Público Press, 1981. 64 pp. Incl. "juan," "tu," "tree," "for," "fi," "seex," "se ven," "e it," "na in," "ten," "ee le ven?," "tú él," "tracy," "birth," "borinquen," "freedom when?," "no bodi?," "felina," "saw," "they's," "nevermind," "squinting," "got," "young fawn," "allow," "yet," "black outs," "shell," " 'tis," "life?," "people," "here," "when in new york," "my," "look up," "a flashlight," "straw mat," "do u remember," "teach not," "i," "why," "contra," "scratching six, plucking one," "dream," "how it is," "been," "get," "cornfields thaw out," and "all over."

5. *Timespace huracán: poems 1972-1975.* Albuquerque, NM: Pajarito Pubs., 1976. Preface, José Armas. 100 pp. Incl. "mujeres de rebozo," "mira," "soledad," "cuetes chispas," "tierras carnes," "calmados," "luna llena," "gusano," "caminando van," "tizoc," "hacendado," "planteando," "miedo," "pa'dar un paso," "la paz," "nubes de lucha," "corazón nos conocemos," "venadito terrenal," "petra/logan '74," "corrido proletario," "inlak'ech," "tiernos murmullos," "ocasos," "silencio'ndo," "todos estamos relacionados," "cristalinos reflejos," "y ranas croares," "fugaces estrellas tropas," "hamacas brisas," "solar alma liberta," "regulation sacrifice," "hummingbirds chupan," "dogs bark cantos," "soft winds," "lunares nubes," "soft breeze," "pinos sway," "pacencia," "round table trabajo," "lucha," "sombras antiguas," "fertil polvo," "wachinton d c," "cadenas rotas," "parque xicano/logan '70," "what it is/is/what it does," "a pelear," "a oír raza," "ollín," "porque," "wild butterflies," "sovereignty," "queletzú, queletzú, queletzú, queletzú," "amerindian circle," "cantares arrullos," "justicia," "infantes corazones," "what for?/pa' victor hara," "adiós, adiós, adiós," "sometime war," "raza unida," and "en amerindia."

B. *Books for children*

6. *Colección Tula y Tonán.* 9 vols. San Diego, CA: Toltecas en Aztlán Publications, 1973.
Incl. *La semilla, El árbol de la vida, El pueblo de colores, La mata de espinas, La calavera, La fortuna, El fruto, El venado,* and *El espejo.*

C. *Poems in journals, magazines, and newspapers*

7. "Got to Be on Time." *Agenda* (National Council of La Raza), 7, 3 (May-June 1977), 13.
8. "Poem in Lieu of Preface." *Aztlán,* 1, 1 (Spring 1970), ix.
9. "Porque los vientos vuelan" and "Wild Butterflies." *Bilingual Review/Revista Bilingüe,* 2, 1-2 (Jan.-Aug. 1975), 173-75.
10. "Cantares arrullos." *Bilingual Review/Revista Bilingüe,* 2, 3 (Sept.-Dec. 1975), 288-91.
11. "Four by Six." *Café Solo,* No. 8 (Spring 1974), p. 5.
12. "Hacendado," "miedo," "planteando," "la paz," "caminando van," and "sé." *Caracol,* 1, 7 (marzo 1975), 12.
13. "Inlakech." *Caracol,* 1, 8 (abril 1975), 20.
14. "Miedo." *Caracol,* 1, 11 (julio 1975), 15.
15. "Borinquen," "Borinquen/dos," "Borinquen/tres," and "Squinting." *Caracol,* 4, 5 (enero 1978), 4.
16. "Let yourself be sidetracked by your güiro." *La Gente* (UCLA), 3, 4 (27 Feb. 1973), 10.
17. "The Poetry of Alurista." *El Grito,* 2, 1 (Fall 1968), 5-12.
Incl. "Mis ojos hinchados," "cantos de ranas viejas," "tarde sobria," "grietas paredes," "nuestro barrio," "must be the season of the witch," "I've been conditioned," "unexpectedly: my night gloom came," "i found a picture," "salsa con crackers," and "can this really be the end."
18. "squinting," "juan," "tu," "tree," "for," and "fi." *El Grito del Sol,* 3, 3 (July-Sept. 1978), 30-32.
19. "Mar de sangres," "Ostia Tortilla," and "El carnalismo nos une." *Hispamérica,* 2, 6 (abril 1974), 95-102.
20. "Tenochtitlán 74: 5º festival de teatros xicanos/Primer encuentro latinoamericano." *Hispamérica,* 3, 8 (1974), 61-64.
21. "Sombras antiguas." *Lemming* (San Diego, CA), No. 7 (Spring 1974), p. 4.
22. "dusk double doors," "clamped almas," "corazón lápida," "lenguagarganta acallecida," and "it is said." *El Leño* (Chicano Dept., San Diego State College), 1968, pp. 1-2, 5.
23. "Siers robo" and "I hate." *Maize,* 1, 1 (Fall 1977), 31, 34.
24. "Caudillo de arena." *Maize,* 1, 2 (Winter 1977), 39.
25. "Corn stalks...." *Maize,* 1, 3 (primavera 1978), front cover.
26. "a," "been," and "cabezeando." *Maize,* 1, 4 (verano 1978), 52-54.
27. "jc's monojog at camp slingshot," "pues," "e it," and "tú él." *Maize,* 2, 2 (Winter 1979), 59-60, inside flaps.
28. "Chuck." *Maize,* 2, 4 (1979), 60.

29. "cornfields thaw out," "all over," and "ms. x." *Maize*, 3, 1-2 (Fall-Winter 1979-80), 66, 68-69.

30. "¿aztlán, quo vadis?" *Maize*, 4, 1-2 (Fall-Winter 1980-81), 64.

31. "Amerindia." *Mester*, 4, 1 (Nov. 1973), 27. Incl. "Mujeres de rebozo" and "Gusano."

32. "nevermind." *Mester*, 6, 2 (mayo 1977), 114.

33. "Pachuco Paz." *New West*, 3, 19 (11 Sept. 1978), 46.

34. "it is said." *Papel Chicano* (Houston, TX), 1, 11 (3 Feb. [1971]), 8.

35. "Bendito sea tu vientre," "Chicano infante," "Cualquier hora," "En la mesa," "In the barrio sopla el viento," "Mis ojos hinchados," and "El pan nuestro." *Papel Chicano* (Houston, TX), 2, 10 (1 June 1972), 8-9.

36. "Nuestro barrio" and "Cabeceando." *Plural*, Segunda época, 8, 96 (Sept. 1979), 7.

37. "Puro pedo" and "Umbilical Chalice." *El Pocho Che*, 1, 1 (Aug. 1969), n.p.*

38. "Offering of Man to God," "The People Bronzed in Sun," and "Turn On." *El Pocho Che*, 1, 2 (1969), 33-34.*

39. "Mis ojos hinchados" (excerpt). *La Raza Habla* (San Diego State College), 27 April 1970, p. 1.

40. "Haikus chicanos." *Revista Chicano-Riqueña*, 2, 1 (invierno 1974), 24.

41. "Life Throbs" and "Black Outs." *RiverSedge*, 2, 2 (1978), 7.

42. "zamna" and "zahi." *Roadwork* (Univ. of California/San Diego), No. 6 (1980), pp. 80-81.

43. "Fascil." *La Semana de Bellas Artes* (México DF), No. 133 (18 junio 1980), p. 13.

44. "Ronnie fast; Ronnie, Ronnie." *Sunrise* (San Diego State College), No. 3 (4 May 1970), p. 2.

45. "la paz," "hacendado," "mujeres de rebozo," "caminando van," and "luna llena." *Tejidos*, 1, 1 (otoño 1973), 15-25.

46. "fascil," "they's," " 'ora," "felina," "juan," "tú," and "tree." *Tejidos*, 4, 2 (verano 1977), 29-33.

47. "Sovereignty." *Tin Tan: Revista Cósmica*, No. 3 (Spring 1976), p. 10.

48. "La cucaracha," "Wheat Paper Cucarachas," "You Have Seen the Cucaracha," and "We've Played Cowboys." *La Verdad* (San Diego, CA), 1, 5 (13 Feb. 1969), 6-7.

49. "En el barrio" and "I Know What Awaits Me." *La Verdad* (San Diego, CA), 1, 6 (March 1969), 3.

50. "Bronze breath." *La Verdad* (San Diego, CA), 1, 9 (June 1969), 8-9.

51. "Run down" and "by the gentle flapping." *La Verdad* (San Diego, CA), 1, 10 (July 1969), 10.

52. "Viet-Nam." *La Verdad* (San Diego, CA), 1, 13 (Oct. 1969), 6.

53. "candle shuffle." *La Verdad* (San Diego, CA), 1, 15 (Dec. 1969), 6.

54. "double dusk doors," "clamped almas," "corazón lápida," and "lengua-garganta acallecida." *La Verdad* (San Diego, CA), No. 18 (March 1970), pp. 14-15.

55. "El carnalismo nos une." *La Verdad* (San Diego, CA), No. 19 bis (May 1970), p. 9.

56. "black hair—maternal shawls." *La Verdad* (San Diego, CA), No. 20 (June 1970), p. 8.

57. "City Manager Hahn: Ping-Pong Eyed." *La Verdad* (San Diego, CA), No. 21 (July 1970), p. 11.

58. "War: power: peace. A letter to Tizoc." *La Verdad* (San Diego, CA), No. 24 (Oct. 1970), pp. 12-13.

59. "Poem" ["hey/hay headed ..."]. *Y'Bird Magazine*, 1, 1 [1977-78], 14.

D. *Poems in anthologies*

60. "Poem in Lieu of Preface" and "Campo Cultural de la Raza." In *Aztlán: An Anthology of Mexican American Literature*. Ed. Luis Valdez and Stan Steiner. New York: Vintage, 1972. Pp. 332-33 and 389-91.

61. "address" and "when raza?" In *Chicano Voices*. Ed. Carlota Cárdenas de Dwyer. Boston: Houghton Mifflin, 1975. Pp. 2, 187.

62. "We've played cowboys," "Mar de sangres," "Ostia tortilla," and "El carnalismo nos une." In *Chicanos: Antología histórica y literaria*. Ed. Tino Villanueva. México: Fondo de Cultura Económica, 1980. Pp. 245-53.

63. "Mis ojos hinchados," "cantos de ranas viejas," "tarde sobria," "grietas paredes," "nuestro barrio," "must be the season of the witch," "I've been conditioned," "unexpectedly: my night gloom came," "i found a picture," "salsa con crackers," and "can this really be the end." In *El Espejo/The Mirror*. Ed. Octavio Ignacio Romano-V. First edition. Berkeley: Quinto Sol Publications, 1969. Pp. 172-78.

64. "Mis ojos hinchados," "cantos de ranas viejas," "grietas paredes," and "unexpectedly: my night gloom came." In *El Espejo/The Mirror*. Ed. Octavio Ignacio Romano-V. and Herminio Ríos C. Fifth printing (revised). Berkeley, CA: Quinto Sol, 1972. Pp. 267-71.

65. "Sombras antiguas," "a oír raza," "independencia y libertad," "la vida o la muerte," "a pelear," "hacendado," "la paz," "caminando van," "what it is/ is/what it does," "mujeres de rebozo," "nubes de lucha," and "luna llena." In *Festival de Flor y Canto: An Anthology of Chicano Literature*. Ed. Alurista, F.A. Cervantes, Juan Gómez-Quiñones, Mary Ann Pacheco and Gustavo Segade. Los Angeles: El Centro Chicano, Univ. of Southern California Press, 1976. Pp. 40-46.

66. Introduction and "Cantares arrullos." In *Festival Flor y Canto II: An Anthology of Chicano Literature from the Festival held March 12-16, 1975, Austin, Texas*. Ed. Arnold C. Vento, Alurista, José Flores Peregrino et al. Albuquerque, NM: Pajarito Pubs., [1979]. Pp. 13-15, 57-60.

67. "It is said." In *Focus on Literature: America* [Vol. 5]. Ed. Philip McFarland, Frances Feagin, Samuel Hay, Stella S.F. Lin, Frank McLaughlin, and Norma Wilson. Boston: Houghton Mifflin, 1978. P. 542.

68. "Mis ojos hinchados." In *From the Belly of the Shark*. Ed. Walter Lowenfels. New York: Vintage, 1973. Pp. 80-81.

69. "Sombras antiguas." In *Humanidad: Essays in Honor of George I. Sánchez*. Ed. Américo Paredes. Los Angeles: Chicano Studies Center Publications, Univ. of California/Los Angeles, 1977. [P. v.]

70. "Raza Unida (lied)." In *Kerstgeschenk van Koffie & Eet Huis "Laurier 33", 1e Laurierdwarsstratt 33*. [Amsterdam, 1980.] P. 6.

71. "We've Played Cowboys," "Must be the Season of the Witch," and "Nuestro barrio." In *Literatura chicana: texto y contexto/Chicano Literature: Text and Context.* Ed. Antonia Castañeda Shular, Tomás Ybarra-Frausto, and Joseph Sommers. Englewood Cliffs, NJ: Prentice-Hall, 1972. Pp. 31-32, 104-05, 157.

72. "the man say we making noise." In *NACLA presents Rius: Los Chicanos.* New York & Berkeley: North American Congress on Latin America, 1972. Back cover.

73. "El carnalismo nos une," "day and fire," "en las montañas," "umbelical chalice," "urban prison," "got to be on time," "las cananas y el calvario," "bronze rape," "face your fears, carnal," "offering of man to god" and "me retiro con mis sueños." In *El Ombligo de Aztlán.* Ed. Alurista and Jorge González. San Diego: Centro de Estudios Chicanos Publications, San Diego State College, 1971. Pp. viii-xi, 6, 8, 19, 29, 40-41, 49, 52, 58, 74-76.

74. "En el núcleo se pasea la mosca," "en el barrio," "en la selva, abandonadas," and "pa' dar un paso." In *Poesía chicana.* Ed. Fernando García Núñez. Material de Lectura, Serie Poesía Moderna 41. México: Departamento de Humanidades, Dirección General de Difusión Cultural, Fondo Nacional para Actividades Sociales, UNAM, n.d. Pp. 5-9.

75. "lo que dentro se mueve," "aguas almendras," "milpas montañas," "lucientes luceros pueblos," "pariyacuah, pariyacuah," "cadensiosos amaneceres," "en la niebla los rostros," "brisa paz a las mares," and "mares resuellan." In *El quetzal emplumece.* Ed. Carmela Montalvo, Leonardo Anguiano, and Cecilio García Camarillo. San Antonio, TX: Mexican American Cultural Center, 1976. Pp. 3-7.

76. "What's happening." In *Three Perspectives on Ethnicity in America: Blacks, Chicanos, and Native Americans.* Ed. Carlos E. Cortés, Arlin I. Ginsburg, Alan W. F. Green, and James A. Joseph. New York: G.P. Putnam's Sons/Capricorn Books, 1976. Pp. 337-38.

77. "Chile ... What For/Song" and "Cuetes Chispas." In *Time to Greez!: Incantations from the Third World.* Ed. Janice Mirikitani et al. San Francisco: Glide Publications & Third World Communications, 1975. Pp. 203-04.

78. "Papeles," "travesiaustin," "oo" ["monopolios/malparidos"], and "acaso." In *Trece Aliens.* N.p.: Trece Aliens, 1976. Pp. 1-4.

79. "When Raza?," "La canería y el sol," "The man has lost his shadow," "Libertad sin lágrimas," "I can't keep from crying," "We and nuestra independencia," "La cucaracha and the crumbs," "nuestra voluntad," "El sarape de mi personalidad," "y mi ego revivar," and "You know that I would be untrue." In *Voices from the Ghetto.* Ed. Arthur Graham. San Diego: A Black Book Production, 1968. Pp. 28-40.

80. "when raza?," "in the barrio sopla el viento," "must be the season of the witch," "en el barrio," "fruto de bronce," and "can this really be the end?" In *Voices of Aztlán: Chicano Literature of Today.* Ed. Dorothy E. Harth and Lewis M. Baldwin. New York: New American Library/Mentor, 1974. Pp. 177-83.

E. Poem issued separately

81. "return." Issued as 4 x 6" card by Mudborn Press, 209 W. De la Guerra,

Santa Barbara, CA.
Rpt. in this volume, p. 138.

F. Short Stories

82. "Moisés come caca de toro." *Caracol*, 2, 11 (julio 1976), 15, 21.
83. "mojologue." *Maize*, 2, 1 (otoño 1978), 36-39.
84. "Mojólogue." In *Calafia: The California Poetry*. Ed. Ishmael Reed. Berkeley: Y'Bird Books, 1979. Pp. 9-12.
85. "Nightmare." *Lit Parade* (San Diego High School), 25 (June 1965), 4.
86. "Trinidad tecata." *Caracol*, 3, 2 (Oct. 1976), 10.

G. Play

87. "Dawn." *El Grito*, 7, 4 (June-Aug. 1974), 55-84.
88. "Dawn." In *Contemporary Chicano Theatre*. Ed. Roberto J. Garza. Notre Dame, IN: Univ. of Notre Dame, 1976. Pp. 103-34.

H. Essays and literary criticism

89. "Alienación e ironía en los personajes de Arlt y Acosta." *El Grito del Sol*, 2, 4 (Oct.-Dec. 1977), 69-80.
90. "*Boquitas Pintadas*: Producción Folletinesca Bajo el Militarismo." *Maize*, 4, 1-2 (Fall-Winter 1980-81), 21-26.
91. "El Capital y su Género: La Novela/ ... Material, Instrumento y Dinero, Producto y Mercado." *Maize*, 3, 3-4 (Spring-Summer 1980), 23-41.
92. "El caso, la novela y la historia en la obra de Acosta: *The Revolt of the Cockroach People*." *Maize*, 2, 3 (primavera 1979), 6-13.
93. "The Chicano Cultural Revolution." *De Colores*, 1, 1 (Winter 1973), 23-33.
94. "La estética indígena a través del Floricanto de Nezahuacóyotl." *Revista Chicano-Riqueña*, 5, 2 (primavera 1977), 48-62.
95. "From Tragedy to Caricature ... and Beyond." *Aztlán*, 11, 1 (Spring 1980), 89-97,
Paper presented at MLA, San Francisco, 1979. On Gregorio Cortez and Oscar Z. Acosta.
See also item 60.

I. Introductions

96. *Get Your Tortillas Together*, by Cecilio García-Camarillo, Carmen Tafolla, and Reyes Cárdenas. N.p., 1976. [Pp. 4-5.]
97. *Space Flutes and Barrio Paths*, by Alex "Gallo" Kirack. San Diego, CA: Centro de Estudios Chicanos Publications [San Diego State Univ.], 1972. P. v.
98. *There Are No Flights Out Tonight*, by Ricardo Teall. Albuquerque, NM: Pajarito Pubs., [1975]. Pp. 9-10.
See also item 66.

II. About Alurista

J. Critical articles and papers

99. Blouin, Egla Morales. "Símbolos y motivos nahuas en la literatura chicana." *Bilingual Review/Revista Bilingüe*, 5, 1-2 (Jan.-Aug. 1978), 99-106.
Rpt. in *The Identification and Analysis of Chicano Literature*. Ed. Francisco Jiménez. New York: Bilingual Press/Editorial Bilingüe, 1979. Pp. 179-90.

100. Bruce-Novoa. "The Expanding Space of Chicano Literature. Update: 1978." Paper presented at Canto al Pueblo, Corpus Christi, TX, 5 June 1978.

101. Bruce-Novoa, John D. "México en la literatura chicana." *Revista de la Universidad de México*, 29, 5 (enero 1975), 13-18.
Rpt. in *Tejidos*, 3, 3 (otoño 1976), 31-42.
Rpt. in *Chicanos: Antología histórica y literaria*. Comp. Tino Villanueva. México: Fondo de Cultura Económica, 1980. Pp. 188-99.

102. Cárdenas de Dwyer, Carlota. " 'address,' by Alurista." In "A Novel (Poem, Story, Essay) to Teach." Comp. Susan Koch. *English Journal*, 65, 1 (Jan. 1976), 63-64.

103. Cárdenas de Dwyer, Carlota. "Chicano Poetry." *Literary Criterion* (Univ. of Mysore, India), 12, 1 (Winter 1975), 23-35.

104. Cárdenas de Dwyer, Carlota. *Chicano Voices: Instructor's Guide*. Boston: Houghton Mifflin, 1975. Pp. 1-3, 91-92.
Accompanies item 61.

105. Cárdenas de Dwyer, Carlota. "Myth and Folk Culture in Contemporary Chicano Literature." *La Luz*, 3, 9 (Dec. 1974), 28-29.
Paper presented at Conference on College Composition and Communications, April 1973.

106. Cárdenas de Dwyer, Carlota. "The Poetics of Code Switching." In *College English and the Mexican American Student*. Ed. Paul Willcott and Jacob Ornstein. San Antonio, TX: Trinity Univ., 1977. Pp. 4-14.
Paper presented at conference of same title, Pan American Univ., Edinburg, TX, 22 Jan. 1976.

107. Elizondo, Sergio. "Alurista: El *Floricanto*, notas sobre la ideología y la poética." Paper presented at Pacific Coast Council on Latin American Studies, San Diego, CA, 27-29 Sept. 1973.

108. Elizondo, Sergio. "Alurista: Metáfora y símbolo." Paper presented at MLA, New York, Dec. 1976.
On sun as principal symbol.

109. Elizondo, Sergio D. "Myth and Reality in Chicano Literature." *Latin American Literary Review*, 5, 10 (Spring-Summer 1977), 23-31.

110. de la Fuente, Patricia. "Themes and Trends in Chicano Poetry: Past, Present and Future." In *Reflections of the Mexican Experience in Texas*. Symposium sponsored by Texas Committee for the Humanities and Mexican American Studies Program, 19-20 April 1979. Ed. Margarita B. Melville and Hilda Castillo Phariss. Monograph No. 1. Houston, TX: Mexican American Studies, Univ. of Houston, 1979. Pp. 154-201. Commentary by Lucy Gonzales, pp. 202-07.

111. Garza, Mario. "Duality in Chicano Poetry." *De Colores*, 3, 4 [1977], 39-45.

112. González, Rafael Jesús. "Pensamientos sobre la literatura chicana." In *Proceedings, National Conference on Bilingual Education April 14-15, 1972.* Austin, TX: Dissemination Center for Bilingual Education, 1972. Pp. 26-39.* Also in *Mujer* (Cd. Juárez, Chih.), 2, 1 (1972).*

113. Hancock, Joel. "The Emergence of Chicano Poetry: A Survey of Sources, Themes and Techniques." *Arizona Quarterly*, 29, 1 (Spring 1973), 57-73.

114. Huerta, Jorge. "From Quetzalcóatl to Honest Sancho: A Review Article of *Contemporary Chicano Theatre.*" *Revista Chicano-Riqueña*, 5, 3 (verano 1977), 32-49.

115. Kanellos, Nicolás. "La Llorona de Alurista." In *Otros mundos, otros fuegos; Fantasía y Realismo Mágico en Iberoamérica* (Memoria del XVI Congreso del Instituto Internacional de Literatura Iberoamericana). Aug. 1973. Ed. Donald A Yates. East Lansing: Michigan State Univ., 1975. Pp. 261-64.

116. Keller, Gary D. "The Literary Strategems Available to the Bilingual Chicano Writer." In *The Identification and Analysis of Chicano Literature.* Ed. Francisco Jiménez. New York: Bilingual Press/Editorial Bilingüe, 1979. Pp. 263-316.

117. Lomelí, Francisco A., and Donaldo W. Urioste. "El concepto del barrio en tres poetas chicanos: Abelardo, Alurista y Ricardo Sánchez." *De Colores*, 3, 4 [1977], 22-29.
Rpt. with English trans. by F. Lomelí and Sonia Zúñiga in *Grito del Sol*, 2, 4 (Oct.-Dec. 1977), 9-24 (Engl.) and 25-38 (Span.).
Paper presented at AATSP, Chicago, 1975. Resumé in *Hispania*, 59, 1 (March 1975), 196.

118. Maldonado, Jesús. *Poesía Chicana: Alurista, el Mero Chingón.* Monograph No. 1. Seattle: Centro de Estudios Chicanos de la Univ. de Washington, 1971. 11 pp.

119. Ortega, Adolfo. "Of Social Politics and Poetry: A Chicano Perspective." *Latin American Literary Review*, 5, 10 (Spring-Summer 1977), 32-41.
Trans. as "Forjando una voz política en la poesía chicana." *Abside*, 42 (1978), 99-115.

120. Ortego, Philip D. "Chicano Poetry: Roots and Writers." In *New Voices in Literature: The Mexican American.* Ed. Edward Simmen. Edinburg, TX: Pan American Univ., 1971. Pp. 1-17.
Rpt. in *Southwestern American Literature*, 2, 1 (Spring 1972), 8-24.
Paper presented at Chicano literature conference, Pan American Univ., 7-8 Oct. 1971.

121. Pérez, Arturo P. "Poesía chicana." *Cuadernos Hispanoamericanos*, No. 325 (julio 1977), pp. 123-131.

122. Pino, Frank. "Chicano Poetry: A Popular Manifesto." *Journal of Popular Culture*, 6, 4 (Spring 1973), 718-30.
Paper presented at Popular Culture Assn., Toledo, OH, April 1972.

123. Robinson, Cecil. "Chicano Literature." In *Mexico and the Hispanic Southwest in American Literature.* (Revised ed. of *With the Ears of Strangers: The Mexican in American Literature*, 1963.) Tucson: Univ. of Arizona, 1977. Pp. 308-31.

124. Robinson, Cecil. "With Ears Attuned—and the Sound of New Voices:

An Updating of *With the Ears of Strangers.*" *Southwestern American Literature,* 1, 2 (May 1971), 51-59.

125. Rodríguez del Pino, Salvador. "La poesía chicana: una nueva trayectoria." In *The Identification and Analysis of Chicano Literature.* Ed. Francisco Jiménez. New York: Bilingual Press/Editorial Bilingüe, 1979. Pp. 68-89.

126. Roeder, Beatrice A. "First Anthology of Chicano Theatre: An Editorial Embarrassment." *Bilingual Review/Revista Bilingüe,* 4, 1-2 (Jan.-Aug. 1977), 151-53.

127. Rojas, Guillermo. "Alurista, Chicano Poet, Poet of Social Protest." In *Otros mundos, otros fuegos; Fantasía y Realismo Mágico en Iberoamérica* (Memoria del XVI Congreso del Instituto Internacional de Literatura Iberoamericana). Aug. 1973. Ed. Donald A. Yates. East Lansing: Michigan State Univ., 1975. Pp. 255-60.

128. Segade, Gustavo. "Chicano Indigenismo: Alurista and Miguel Méndez." *Xalmán,* 1, 4 (Spring 1977), 4-11.

129. Testa, Daniel. "Alurista: Three Attitudes Toward Love in His Poetry." *Revista Chicano-Riqueña,* 4, 1 (invierno 1976), 46-55.
Paper presented at Conference on Twentieth Century Literature, Univ. of Louisville (KY), 28 Feb.-2 March 1974.

130. Torres, Luis. "Relevance in Chicano Literature." *Metamorfosis* (Univ. of Washington, Seattle), 1, 1 (1977), 36-40.
Paper read at Rocky Mountain MLA, Las Vegas, NV, 22 Oct. 1977.
Abstract in *Rocky Mountain Review of Language and Literature,* 31, 3 (Summer 1977), 150.

131. Valdés Fallis, Guadalupe. "Code-switching in bilingual Chicano poetry." *Hispania,* 59, 4 (Dec. 1976), 877-86.
Rpt. from *Southwest Languages and Linguistics in Educational Perspective.* Proceedings of the Third Annual Southwest Areal Languages and Linguistics Workshop, Northern Arizona University, Flagstaff, AZ, April 1974. Ed. Gina Cantoni Harvey and M. F. Heiser. San Diego, CA: Institute for Cultural Pluralism, San Diego State University, 1975. Pp. 143-60. Discussion by David William Foster, pp. 161-70.

132. Valdés Fallis, Guadalupe. "The Sociolinguistics of Chicano Literature: Towards an Analysis of the Role and Function of Language Alternation in Contemporary Bilingual Poetry." Paper presented at MLA, New York, 27 Dec. 1976.
Shorter version in *Punto de Contacto/Point of Contact,* 1, 4 (1977), 30-39.

133. Vento, Arnold C. "Exponentes recientes de la literatura chicana en lengua hispánica." Paper presented at MLA, Chicago, 28 Dec. 1977, and at Canto al Pueblo, Corpus Christi, TX, 5 June 1978.

134. Villanueva, Tino. "Apuntes sobre la poesía chicana." *Papeles de Son Armadans,* Nos. 271-73 (oct.-dic. 1978), pp. 41-70.
Rpt. in *Chicanos: Antología histórica y literaria.* Comp. Tino Villanueva. México: Fondo de Cultura Económica, 1980. Pp. 48-67.

135. Ybarra-Frausto, Tomás. "Alurista's Poetics: The Oral, The Bilingual, The Pre-Columbian." In *Modern Chicano Writers.* Ed. Joseph Sommers and Tomás Ybarra-Frausto. Englewood Cliffs, NJ: Prentice-Hall, 1979. Pp. 117-32.

ERNESTINA N. EGER

K. Dissertations and theses

136. Aguilar-Henson, Marcella. "Chicano poetry: an international and personal search for identity." Diss. in progress at Univ. of New Mexico.
137. Cárdenas de Dwyer, Carlota. "Chicano Literature 1967-75: The Flowering of the Southwest." *DAI*, 37, 3 (Sept. 1976), 1582-83A.
138. Córdova, Robert Herman. "Syntax and Bilingual Chicano Poetry." *DAI*, 38, 12 (June 1978), 7359-60A.
139. Sedano, Michael Victor. "Chicanismo in Selected Poetry from the Chicano Movement, 1969-1972: A Rhetorical Study." *DAI*, 41, 4 (Oct. 1980), 1281-82A.
140. Vogel, Cathleen. "Alurista: Chicano Poet, Universal Voice." Unpublished MA thesis. Bradley Univ., 1980. iv + 101 pp.
141. Ybarra-Frausto, Tomás. "Three Contemporary Chicano Poets: Antecedents and Actuality." *DAI*, 40, 6 (Dec. 1979), 3348A.*

L. Reviews and bibliographic annotations

142. "Chicano Book Review." *Inside the Beast* (San Diego State Univ.), 1, 6 (15 Jan. 1973), 4.
Incl. *El Ombligo de Aztlán* and *Nationchild Plumaroja*.
143. Hancock, Joel. Review of *Floricanto en Aztlán*. *Modern Language Journal*, 56, 3 (March 1972), 181-82.
144. Lomelí, Francisco A., and Donaldo W. Urioste. *Chicano Perspectives in Literature: A Critical and Annotated Bibliography*. Albuquerque, NM: Pajarito Publications, 1976.
145. Lomelí, Francisco A., and Donaldo W. Urioste. Review of *Timespace Huracán*. *De Colores*, 3, 4 [1977], 83.
Rpt. from item 144.
146. Rodríguez, Juan. "Reseña Crítica: A Review of Alurista's Poetry Reading at UCSD." *El Sol* (Center for Iberian and Latin American Studies, Univ. of California/San Diego), 1, 1 (16 Oct. 1975), 6.
147. Shirley, Carl D. "The Search for Chicano Identity: A Definitive Survey." *Hispania*, 59, 2 (May 1976), 394-96.
Rpt. in *MELUS* [Newsletter], 3, 4 (Winter 1976), 24-26.
Incl. items 184 and 185.
148. [Sonntag, Iliana.] Review of *Timespace Huracán: Poems 1972-75*. *Books of the Southwest*, No. 239 (Oct. 1978), p. 1.
149. Tatum, Charles M. *A Selected and Annotated Bibliography of Chicano Studies*. Manhattan, KS: Kansas State Univ., Society of Spanish and Spanish-American Studies, 1976.
Second edition. Lincoln, NE: Univ. of Nebraska, SSSAS, Modern Languages and Literatures, 1979.

M. Interviews

150. Anguiano, Marco. "Interview With Alurista." *Community Arts Newsletter* (San Diego, CA), 2, 5 (May 1980), 5.
151. Bruce-Novoa, [Juan]. "Alurista." In *Chicano Authors: Inquiry by Inter-*

view. Austin and London: Univ. of Texas Press, 1980. Pp. 265-87.

152. "Culture as a Weapon: an interview with Alurista." *La Verdad* (San Diego, CA), No. 23 (Sept. 1970), p. 9.

153. Engstrom, Carla. "Love is motivating force for poet in Chicano revolution." *Daily Nebraskan* (Univ. of Nebraska, Lincoln), 8 March 1978, p. 8.

154. Gómez, Linda. "Alurista 'A mirror of the people's heart'." *El Mundo* (Oakland, CA), 15, 97 (17 dic. 1975), 3.

155. Levine, Joan. " 'Poet of the Future' Cherishes Hispanic Past." *San Diego* (CA) *Union*, 6 July 1979, pp. D 1-2.

156. Milkowski, Bill. "Poet Hails Latin Push for Identity." *Milwaukee Journal*, 18 July 1976, Sec. 2, p. 9.

157. Mulder, Reinjan. "Ik ben een dichter, geen held." *NRC Handelsblad* (Amsterdam, Holland), Cultureel Supplement 527, 28 Nov. 1980.

158. Mundth, Michelle. "Nonprofit poet views craft: Writes to preserve sanity." *Daily Aztec* (San Diego State Univ.), 56, 59 (14 Dec. 1976), 4.

Rpt. in *Papeles de la Frontera*, Feb. 1977, pp. 4-5.

159. Ruffinelli, Jorge. "Alurista: Una larga marcha hacia Aztlán." *La palabra y el hombre* (Univ. Veracruzana), Nueva época, Núm. 17 (enero-marzo 1976), pp. 30-41.

Rpt. in *El lugar de Rulfo y otros ensayos*. Xalapa: Biblioteca, Univ. Veracruzana, 1980. Pp. 201-17.

160. Smith, Gordon. "Two Poets." *Reader: San Diego's Weekly*, 7, 24 (22 June 1978).

On Alurista and Pedro Ortiz-Vásquez, editor of *Citybender*.

161. Vara, Richard. " 'Alurista' never thinking of slowing his hectic pace." *Houston Post*, 29 Feb. 1976, p. 4D.

See also item 186.

N. News articles

162. "Authors, publishers here for National Latino Book Fair." *Houston Chronicle*, 6 Nov. 1980, Sec. 5 (Weekend Preview), pp. 1, 6.

163. Avendaño, Luis G. "Los problemas de la comunidad chicana a través de la expresión artística, hoy en la Casa del Lago." *Uno más Uno* (México DF), 22 Oct. 1978, p. 17.

164. Balderrama, Guillermo. "Un grupo de artistas vino a dar prueba de la cultura chicana: Por medio de la música y la poesía nos hablan de sus experiencias." *El Día* (México DF), ca. 18 Oct. 1978, Sec. "Divertimientos."

165. "Chicano poet due at SDSU." *Imperial Valley Press* (El Centro, CA), 30 Aug. 1980.*

166. "Declamará sus poesías laureado poeta." *La Voz de Houston*, 12 marzo 1981, p. 3.

167. "First Chicano poetry reading." *La Verdad* (San Diego, CA), No. 27 (April 1971), p. 9.

168. Keen, Harold. "The Death of Tío Taco." *San Diego Magazine*, 22, 10 (Aug. 1970), pp. 94-99, 103, 113, 116, 118.

On San Diego Chicano community, with photo and some mention of Alurista.

ERNESTINA N. EGER

169. Murphy, Patricia Lee. "Artists Renew Toltecas Crafts Heritage." *Los Angeles Times*, 23 May 1971, Sec. E, p. 10.
On Toltecas en Aztlán, with photo of Alurista.
170. Neussendorfer, Margaret. "A Festival of American Poetry." *Texas Books in Review*, 1, 1 [1977], 23.
Participants incl. Alurista.
171. Novo de Pena, Silvia. "Raíces Históricas del Mexicoamericano. Alurista: Cantor de la Raza." *La Voz de Houston*, 12 marzo 1981, p. 5.
172. O'Neill, Brian. "The Chicano Experience in Higher Education." *Projection* (San Diego State Univ.), 1, 2 (March-April 1972), 19-24.
Incl. Alurista.
173. "Poet to Perform at UNO." *World-Herald* (Omaha, NE), 22 April 1979, "Entertainment" [magazine], p. 9.
174. Rojas Zea, Rodolfo. "El Movimiento Chicano de EU usa la 'Guerrilla Cultural' Para un Cambio Social en el Mundo." *Excelsior* (México DF), 27 junio 1974, p. 11-B.
175. Sotomayor, Frank. "An Explosion of Chicano Literary Merit." *Los Angeles Times*, 28 Jan. 1973, "Calendar," pp. 1, 56, 66.
Rpt. in *La Luz*, 2, 1 (April 1973), 52-53.
Trans. as "Literatura, un Arma en Manos del Movimiento Chicano: Líderes de la 'Raza' que Actúan en Alto Nivel Intelectual." *Novedades* (México DF), 5 feb. 1973, pp. 1, 8.
176. "Toltecas en Aztlán celebrate first Toltecayotl." *La Verdad*, No. 27 (April 1971), p. 3.
Incl. photo of Alurista only.

O. Biographical listings

177. *Contemporary Authors*. Vols. 45-48 (1974), 17.
178. *A Directory of American Poets, 1975 Edition*. New York: Poets and Writers, Inc., 1974. P. 3.
179. Kay, Ernest, ed. *The International Who's Who in Poetry*. Fourth ed., 1974-75. Cambridge and London, England: Melrose Press, 1974. P. 474.
180. Martínez, Julio A., ed. *Chicano Scholars and Writers: A Bio-Bibliographical Directory*. Metuchen, NJ: Scarecrow Press, 1979. Pp. 15-18.

III. Other sources

P. Archive

181. Flores, María G., comp. *Mexican American Archives at the Benson Collection: A Guide for Users*. Ed. Laura Gutiérrez-Witt. Austin: Univ. of Texas at Austin, The General Libraries, 1981.
Pp. 2-4 give narrative summary and inventory of Alurista manuscripts and papers, 1968-79.

154

Q. Audio- and videotapes

182. *Alurista* [sound recording]. Los Angeles: Public Broadcasting, Univ. of Southern California, 1974.
From Festival de Flor y Canto I. Side 2 has recording of Juan Gómez-Quiñones.

183. *Alurista* [video recording]. Festival de Flor y Canto, No. 33. Los Angeles: Division of Public Broadcasting, Univ. of Southern California, 1974. Cassette, 20 min.

184. *Alurista: poet of Aztlán* [sound recording]. Center for Cassette Studies, 1974, No. 35314, 60 min.

185. Alurista and Dorinda Moreno. *Chicano Art: A Renaissance* [sound recording]. Center for Cassette Studies, [1974], No. 34166, 36 min.

186. Rodríguez del Pino, Salvador. *Interview with Alurista* [video recording]. Encuentro with Chicano Poets series. Santa Barbara: Center for Chicano Studies, Univ. of California, 1977. Cassette, 30 min.

CARTHAGE COLLEGE